Hai, Ima!

Workbook

TRUDI SAMPSON   JUNKO GLYNN

Visit the *Hai, Ima!* website at http://www.cisheinemann.com.au/haiima/

First published 2002 by CIS•Heinemann
A division of Reed International Books Australia Pty Ltd
22 Salmon St, Port Melbourne, Victoria 3207
Telephone (03) 9245 7111
Facsimile (03) 9245 7333
World Wide Web http://www.cisheinemann.com.au
Email info@hi.com.au

Offices in Sydney, Brisbane, Adelaide and Perth.
Associated companies, branches and representatives around the world.

2009	2008	2007	2006	2005	2004	2003	2002
8	7	6	5	4	3	2	1

© Reed International Books Australia Pty Ltd 2002

All rights reserved.
No part of this publication may be produced, stored in a retrieval system, or transmitted in any form or by any means, electronic, mechanical, photocopying, recording or otherwise, without prior written permission of the publisher.

Commissioned by Catriona McKenzie
Edited by Anne Gugger
Designed by Kae Sato-Goodsell
Illustrations by Tomomi Sarafov
Map p 54 by Yuki Wada
Series consultant: Sue Burnham
Language consultant: Matt Hagino
Teaching consultant: Karin Ruff
Production by Michelle Sweeney

Film supplied by Typescan
Printed in Australia by Sands Print Group Ltd

Acknowledgements
The publisher wishes to thank the following organisations who kindly gave permission to reproduce copyright material in this book:
p 22 (car navigator system) Permission by Kenwood Corporation.
p 22 (mobile phone) Permission by NTT DoCoMo Inc. i-mode is a trademark or registered trademark of NTT DoCoMo, Inc. in Japan and other countries. © 2002 NTT DoCoMo Inc. All rights reserved.
p 22 (digital video camera) Supplied by Sony corporation.
p 27 (Kirin drink) Permission by Kirin Beverage Corporation.
p 28 (Xbox logo) Supplied by Microsoft.
Despite every effort, the publishers were not successful in contacting every copyright owner prior to going to print. Should this come to the attention of those concerned, the publishers request that they contact them so that proper acknowledgement can be made in any reprint of this book.

もくじ

はじめに		Introduction	iv
Unit 1	わたし	I, me, myself	1
Unit 2	ほしいもの	Things you want	17
Unit 3	しゅうまつ	Weekend	35
Unit 4	あるこう広島(しま)	Visiting Hiroshima	53
Unit 5	トラベル	Travel	69
Unit 6	Myしょう来	Future	87
クイズのこたえ		Quiz solutions	101
Vocabulary	日本語 – 英語		102
	英語 – 日本語		105

はじめに

This *Workbook* has lots of interesting activities to help you practise what you learn in the はい、いま！ *Textbook*. You'll write a profile of a sportsperson for your school magazine, reply to a Japanese email, read some メール on a Japanese mobile phone, follow a mystery tour through the streets of Hiroshima, listen and respond to an interview in Japanese for a part-time job, and lots more.

Most of the activities in this *Workbook* are organised under the same headings as the *Textbook* so you will find it easy to navigate between the two. Each unit begins with a discussion about the 'magazine' cover for that unit, so be ready to look closely, think laterally and share your opinions. Then it's on to たんご and かんじ to familiarise yourself with new vocabulary and kanji before working on the どうぞ presenter pages. In these, you practise new language through drills before applying it in various situations, working individually, in pairs or in small groups.

Once you are familiar with the new language, you'll feel ready to work through とくしゅう and つかってみよう, which contain activities where you can show off your skills. You will also see which indicates occasions when you can use the computer for research or to enhance the presentation of your work.

The おしゃべり activities will help you understand the casual speech style used by your Japanese friends – perfect preparation for when you communicate with them or for exchange visits.

A self-correcting クイズ at the end of each unit gives you the chance to check how well you have understood the new vocabulary, kanji and grammar, and includes suggestions on how to improve.

Throughout the *Workbook* there are helpful hints, and ideas for working smarter rather than longer. There are models to guide you when writing, note taking space to jot down words when listening to the *Audio CDs*, and many hints to develop your learning skills, such as *"Before you listen think about the words you can expect to hear"*.

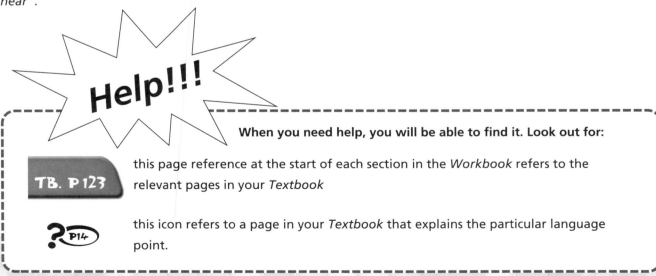

As you know from the introduction to the *Textbook*, each unit is presented as a different 'magazine'.

- Look through the *Textbook* for the title of each 'magazine'.
- Looking at the first 'magazine' read the titles of the sections for vocabulary, new kanji, examples of new grammar, explanations of new grammar, speaking activities, reading activities and explanations of plain form used in casual speech.

Discuss the following as you look at the cover of 「わたし」 on page 1 of the *Textbook*.

- The title of this 'magazine' is 「わたし」. What does this mean? Can you find the kanji for it? Think of three topics you would expect to be included in a magazine like this.
- Magazines usually have a feature article (とくしゅう). What is the とくしゅう of this 'magazine'?
- What do you think メル友 means?
- Who do you think the おしゃれなすいえいのチャンピオン might be?
- Look carefully at the girl. How old do you think she is? What is a possible name for her? Think of some adjectives to describe her appearance.

たんご   TB. P2

Complete the sentences with the appropriate form of the verb indicated by the English phrases.

a 父はひまなとき、バイオリンを _____ 。 (plays)

b きのう、てがみを _____ 。 (wrote)

c おはしを _____ 。 (let's use)

d わたしはフランス語を _____ 。 (don't speak)

e 友だちのうちでCDを _____ 。 (shall we listen?)

2

Complete the crossword in hiragana, using the English hints provided.

よこ

1. animal horoscope
3. meat
4. sociable
5. joke
6. cheerful/bright
8. trendy/fashionable
9. serious
11. come
12. strict
14. go

たて

1. reading
2. quiet/reserved
4. kind
6. intelligent/smart
7. run
10. etc.
13. now

> Make a set of flashcards using small squares of cardboard. Whenever you learn a new word, write a flashcard for it straight away. Carry the set with you in a pocket or pencil case and look at the cards while you're waiting for the train or instead of watching the ads on TV!

第一課 二

かんじ

TB. P3

3

Practise writing these new kanji in the boxes provided.

私							
高							
話							
読							
書							
聞							

! Here are some suggestions for learning and remembering new kanji.

- Try to link new characters with others that you already know.
  E.g. The characters 語 and 話 have the same part on the left, and both have something to do with speaking.

- Try to associate a new character with a picture or story.
  E.g. I'm looking at a tall building.

Maybe you already use techniques like these or you can suggest some others. Try them and find one that suits you.

三 第一課

4 　書

Select an appropriate word from the box and write it under the matching picture.

> 話します　聞きます　読みます　書きます　高校　私

一

高　校
_____

二

_____

三

_____

四

_____

五

_____

六

_____

5 　書

Rewrite these sentences, using kanji for the underlined hiragana.

ⓐ　<u>わたし</u>はよく<u>にほんご</u>の<u>ほん</u>を<u>よみ</u>ます。　_____

ⓑ　ぼくはてがみを<u>かき</u>ません。　_____

ⓒ　<u>えいご</u>で<u>はなし</u>てください。　_____

ⓓ　<u>はは</u>のしゅみは<u>どくしょ</u>です。　_____

ⓔ　このCDを<u>きき</u>ましょう。　_____

ⓕ　<u>あね</u>は<u>せ</u>が<u>たかい</u>です　_____

第一課　四

メル友

TB. P4-5

6 📝

In your exercise book, sort the following group of adjectives into two wide columns of い and な adjectives. Then write the English meaning next to each Japanese word. Check your work with a classmate.

> とくい　しゃこうてき　かっこいい　おしゃれ　ながい　げん気
> シャイ　おとなしい　せがひくい　しんせつ　きびしい　クリエイティブ
> きれい　いい　あかるい　みじかい　高い　まじめ　へん　かわいい

7 📝 ❓P14

PART A

In the space provided, join each pair of adjectives. Remember to apply the rules for い adjectives and な adjectives.

ⓐ かみがみじかい、かわいい _____

ⓑ きれい、げん気 _____

ⓒ おもしろい、スポーツがとくい _____

ⓓ クリエイティブ、あたまがいい _____

PART B

Create your own sentences using a pair of joined adjectives.

ⓐ 私のペットは _____ です。

ⓑ 友だちの _____ さんは

_____ です。

8 🎧

Listen to two students talking about their friends. Circle the adjectives used to describe each friend.

ⓐ　quiet　　　friendly　　serious　　　shy
ⓑ　bright　　sociable　　serious　　　kind
ⓒ　friendly　　bright　　kind　　　creative
ⓓ　intelligent　tall　　fashionable　sociable

> ❗ Before you listen, check you know the Japanese for these words.

Listen to three Japanese teenage friends reading aloud each other's emails before sending them to 「わたし」 magazine. Listen for the key points to complete the following table in English.

 The first time you listen, make a note of any key words in English or Japanese. The next time focus on any gaps. When you have finished, check what you have written and make any changes.

Name	Personality	Likes/skills
けい子		
けんじ		
まり		

10

たろう's introduction has been published in 「わたし」 magazine. Read his message and make notes as indicated in **a ~ d** below.

ぼくはたろうで、日本人の高校生です。おんがくが大好きで、ひまなとき、ギターをひきます。ピアノがとくいです。ぼくはせが高くて、めがねをかけています。おとなしくてまじめです。メールを書いてください。

taroo@ntt.jp

a たろう tells us his name **and** his year level. Circle the part that means 'and'.

b What is たろう's strong point? Underline the sentence which describes his strong point.

c たろう tells us two things about his appearance. Write the English meaning of both these things in the margin.

d たろう describes his personality. Highlight the words he uses and write the English meaning in the margin.

11

Write your own introduction in Japanese for inclusion in the keypal page of 「わたし」. Present your introduction like those on page 4 of the *Textbook* either in Microsoft Word or on paper. Include details such as …

- Your name, age, year level
- Personality
- Appearance
- Hobbies
- Strong points
- A photograph and an email address (Make one up if you prefer)

When you are finished, swap with a partner and check each other's work.

高校生１００人に聞きました… TB. P6-7

12

Rewrite the following verbs in potential form.

a) 書きます　_____　　d) つかいません　_____

b) 読みます　_____　　e) はしりません　_____

c) およぎます　_____　　f) 話しません　_____

13

PART A.

Listen to six people talk about their abilities. Draw a line to match the number of the person with the things they can do.

- Person 1 • • I can sing French songs.
- Person 2 • • I can write kanji beautifully.
- Person 3 • • I can speak English a little bit.
- Person 4 • • I can play the guitar, piano and violin.
- Person 5 • • I can make delicious chocolate cakes and sushi.
- Person 6 • • I can swim one kilometre.

> ! You'll find it easier if you read all the sentences first.

PART B.

Which things listed above can you do? Write them in Japanese in your exercise book, or write three new sentences about things you can do. Then tell your partner the things you can do.

14

Tom and さち子 are talking during lunchtime. Listen to their conversation and circle whether each statement is true (**T**) or false (**F**), according to the information you hear.

a. さち子 has finished her homework.   T   F
b. さち子 cannot read English books.   T   F
c. Cathy cannot speak Japanese, but she can write kanji.   T   F
d. Cathy is clever and serious.   T   F
e. Tom can write kanji.   T   F

> ❗ To make it easier, read all the statements before you start and note down the key Japanese words to listen for. Remember to check your work at the end.

15

「わたし」 magazine is running a competition in which entrants are required to write about their friends. The best entry will win a subscription to the magazine.

PART A

Liz has prepared most of her entry for the competition, but she needs help to finish it. Read what she has done so far. Then in your exercise book, write out what she needs to know to finish it properly.

a. Write the Japanese for the words Liz wrote in English.
b. Write the kanji for the underlined hiragana.
c. Change the verbs 話します and はしります into their potential forms.

> 私は友だちがたくさんいます。いい友だちはフィオナとジャックとえりです。
>
> フィオナは<u>め</u>が大きくて、きれいです。bright and あたまがいいです。フランスごを <u>話します</u>。
>
> ジャックは tall and かみがながいです。おんがくが<u>だいすき</u>で、バイオリンがひけます。おもしろくて、ちょっとへんな boy です。
>
> えりは this year 日本からきました。かみがみじかくて、かわいい<u>ひと</u>です。しゃこうてきで、kind です。スポーツが good at ..., and スキーができます。そして、はやく<u>はしります</u>。

PART B

Draw a chart, like the one below, in your exercise book and complete the information about Liz's three friends in English.

Name	Appearance	Personality	Abilities

Ian Thorpe   TB. P8-9

16

Complete the following table. The first verb has been done for you.

English	～ます form	～ません form	Potential	Negative potential
buy	かいます	かいません	かえます	かえません
stand	たちます			
make			つくれます	
		のみません		
			話せます	
		ねません		
			でかけられます	
wear	きます			
come	きます			
	べんきょうします	べんきょうしません		

17

Use particles from the list to complete the following sentences, according to the English meanings. Particles may be used more than once.

が　の　に　を　や

(a) 私はバレエ _____ とくいです。   I am good at ballet.

(b) 友だち _____ さち子さんはしんせつな人です。   My friend, Sachiko, is a kind person.

(c) ひらがなとかんじ _____ 書けます。   I can write hiragana and kanji.

(d) 土曜日 _____ まち _____ 行って、ようふく _____ ざっしなど _____ かいました。
On Saturday, I went to the city and bought clothes and magazines etc.

18

Look at the feature about Ian Thorpe on page 8 of the *Textbook*. Then complete the following tasks.

a Nine of the katakana words from page 8 are hidden horizontally and vertically in the following puzzle. When you have found them, use the remaining seven characters to spell another word from page 8 and then write the English meaning.

ア	プ	ロ	フ	ィ	ー	ル
イ	フ	テ	ニ	ス	チ	イ
ス	メ	ー	ト	ル	ャ	ア
ク	ポ	ス	タ	ー	ン	ン
リ	リ	リ	マ	ー	ピ	ソ
ー	ス	レ	ン	タ	オ	ー
ム	イ	ー	ゴ	ル	ン	プ

Mystery word: _____

English meaning: _____

b How is Ian described in this article? List three or four points in Japanese and English, writing your answers in your exercise book.

c According to the journalist, what can Ian do? Answer in Japanese, in your exercise book.

d What evidence is there of Ian's popularity in Japan? Answer in English, in your exercise book.

19

a Look at the プロフィール of Ian Thorpe on page 8 of 「わたし」. Answer the following questions in your exercise book using complete Japanese sentences.

1　イアンさんは日本語が話せますか。

2　どこに住んでいますか。

3　たん生日(じょう)はいつですか。

4　好きな食べものは何ですか。(Use や in your answer.)

b Your little sister is a huge fan of Ian Thorpe. She is looking at the Ian Thorpe page in 「わたし」 and is pestering you to tell her what it all says. Write a summary in English of the section titled 「イアン・ソープさんをしょうかいします」 for her.

c Look at the fan-mail at the bottom of page 8. What questions did the fans ask? Write the meaning of each question in your exercise book.

第一課

20

Create a page for your school magazine or website featuring a skillful swimmer or sportsperson at your school. You can refer to questions 18 and 19 on page 11 in this *Workbook* and page 8 of the *Textbook* for ideas of what you could include.

Getting Started

- **First,** think how you want to present your information, for example, as a profile, an article and/or headlines. Then…
- **Decide** who you will write about.
- **Gather** the information you will need, such as name, birthday, place of residence, physical description, personality, what they can do, their likes (food, music, school subjects).
- **Collect** photographs or illustrations that you want to include.
- **Write** a draft in Japanese.
- **Check** your work, or ask a friend to check it for you.
- **Present** your final piece either on paper or using Microsoft Word, Power Point, Publisher or similar software.

Some extra vocabulary to help you …

Football	フットボール	Trophy	トロフィー	Relay	リレー
Tennis	テニス	Ground/oval	うんどうじょう／グランド	Hurdles	ハードル
Soccer	サッカー	Goal	ゴール	Pole vault	ぼうたかとび
Netball	ネットボール	Shoot/score a goal	ゴールイン（です）	Shot put	ほうがんなげ
Hockey	ホッケー	Goal keeper	ゴール・キーパー	Long jump	はしりはばとび
Volleyball	バレーボール	Kick	けります	High jump	はしりたかとび
Basketball	バスケットボール	Singles	シングル	Triple jump	さんだんとび
Athletics	りくじょうきょうぎ	Doubles	ダブルス	Breast stroke	ひらおよぎ
Rowing	ボートレース	A serve	サービス	Back stroke	せおよぎ
Yachting	ヨットきょうそう	Serve	サーブ（を）します	Butterfly	バタフライ
Aerobics	エアロビクス	100 metre event	百メートルきょうそう	Diving	とびこみ
Downhill skiing	スキー	Long distance event	マラソン	Medley Relay	メドレーリレー
Cross country skiing	クロスカントリー・スキー				

とくしゅう

TB. P 12-13

21

Follow the instructions on page 12 of the *Textbook* to work out your animal horoscope. Then find a friend with a different animal sign to you and work together to write a summary in English of both your animal signs, in your exercise book.

22

a) Read the animal horoscopes on page 13 of the *Textbook* and circle the characteristics which apply to these signs. There may be more than one.

Cheetah:	cool	quiet	trendy	smart
Raccoon Dog:	healthy	cheerful	kind	trendy
Pegasus:	kind	fashionable	reserved	smart
Wolf:	cheerful	serious	smart	strict

b) Read the horoscope for Koalas. Then circle まる (true) or ばつ (false) for the following statements.

- They are quiet people.　　　まる　　ばつ
- They like going to the beach.　　まる　　ばつ
- They can eat a lot of fish.　　まる　　ばつ
- They like to study.　　　　まる　　ばつ

c) Complete the horoscope translation for Lions.

Lions are _____ people. They love _____ and can eat a lot.

They can _____ two kilometres. They don't like cleaning, so _____.

d) For Leopard, Baby Deer **or** Tiger, design an emblem in your exercise book which demonstrates at least two of the key characteristics in pictures or symbols.

e) Who am I?

Think about what you know about sheep, elephants and monkeys. Then, keeping that in mind, listen carefully to these horoscopes. Write the number of the appropriate description beside each animal. Be prepared to explain the reason for your decision.

( )　　　( )　　　( )　

第一課　十二

つかってみよう

23

Read the following letter to your class from とし子, who will be studying at your school from next month. Complete the tasks below.

日本語のクラスのみなさんへ

　今日は。私の名前はとし子で、高校一年生です。せがひくくて、かみが みじかいです。あかるくて、しゃこうてきです。どうぶつうらないはチーター です。みなさんは？

　私はスポーツが大好きです。まい日、学校のプールでおよぎます。500メート ルおよげます。テニスもとくいです。テニスぶのメンバーで、まいしゅう土曜日 にしあいをします。私のチームはつよくて、ことしのチャンピオンです。 みなさんはスポーツが好きですか。

　私は英語が好きです。英語の本をよく読みます。でも、あまり話せません。 英語のせんせいはしんせつな人です。みなさんの英語のせんせいは どんな人ですか。

　らい月、私はみなさんの学校で、べんきょうします。どんな学校ですか。 きびしいですか。学生は何人ですか。プールやテニスコートがありますか。 テニスぶはつよいですか。

　てがみを書いてください。たのしみにしています。

　　　　　　　　　　　　　　　　　　さようなら

３月１５日

　　　　　　　　　　　　　　　　　　とし子より

(a) In the letter, とし子 asks you eight questions. Underline them.

(b) Are there words in the letter which you do not know? Circle them. Check the vocabulary list on pages 102 – 108 of this *Workbook*.

(c) In the margin, close to each question, write the key words to include in your answers.

(d) Write a reply to とし子. Follow the model given on the next page to set out your letter correctly. Aim to write about 150 字 (characters).

Letter Writing Style: 手紙のマナー

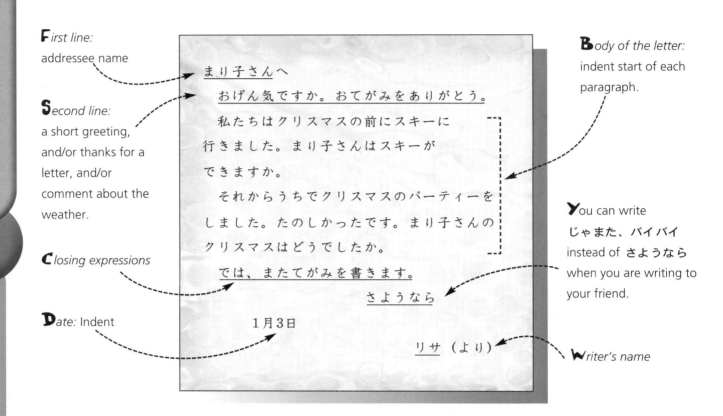

First line: addressee name

Second line: a short greeting, and/or thanks for a letter, and/or comment about the weather.

Closing expressions

Date: Indent

Body of the letter: indent start of each paragraph.

You can write じゃまた、バイバイ instead of さようなら when you are writing to your friend.

Writer's name

おしゃべり　　TB P 16-17

24

Read about *plain form* on page 16 of the *Textbook* and decide whether the following statements are True (**T**) or False (**F**).

a) The plain form is used in casual speech style.　　**T**　　F

b) Casual speech style ends in 〜ます and です.　　T　　**F**

c) Friends, who know each other well, usually use casual speech style.　　**T**　　F

d) です is usually omitted in casual speech style.　　**T**　　F

e) Particles are never omitted in casual speech style.　　T　　**F**

25

Rewrite the following sentences in casual speech style as if part of a conversation between friends.

a このシャツはかっこいいですね。 _____

b そうですね。 _____

c あ！見てください。あのジーンズもすてきですね。 _____

d どこですか。 _____

e あそこです。いすのうしろです。 _____

26

Jessica and ゆか are talking at a party.

PART A.

Fill in the speech bubbles by changing the conversation below each frame into the casual speech style. (ゆか speaks first.)

ゆか: わあ、あの人はせが高くて、ハンサムですね。だれですか。
ジェシカ: あの人はトムさんです。

ゆか: トムさんはどんな人ですか。
ジェシカ: まじめで、おとなしい人です。バスケットボールがじょうずです。

PART B.

Now act out this conversation with a partner.

クイズ！

When you have completed the 「わたし」 unit, try this quiz to see how well you have mastered the key vocabulary, kanji and grammar.

A Complete the following chart. (14 marks)

英語	かんじ	ひらがな	英語	かんじ	ひらがな
I / me	私	わたし	write		
expensive, tall				聞きます	
	話します				こうこうせい
		よみます		読書	

B The best alternative is … (3 marks)

1　ひまなとき、ギターを　（ひきます。話します。あそびます。）

2　よる、本を　（聞きます。飲みます。読みます。）

3　学校でコンピューターを　（書きます。つかいます。はしります。）

C Write the following descriptions in Japanese. (8 marks)

1　めぐみ is tall and pretty. _____

2　たけひと is trendy and has long hair. _____

3　ゆうすけ is smart and sociable. _____

4　ゆみ is shy and quiet. _____

D Write the following sentences in Japanese. Include any kanji you have learnt. (10 marks)

1　Can you use chopsticks? _____

2　Can you eat sashimi? _____

3　I can study on the bus. _____

4　I can run 10 km. _____

5　I can speak German. _____

Check your answers against those on page 101. Give yourself a score and read the assessment at the bottom of the page.

第一課　十六

ほしいもの

The 'magazine' 「ほしいもの」 on page 19 of the *Textbook* is all about Japanese hi-tech goods.

How much do you know about hi-tech Japan? Using a full page in your exercise book, brainstorm a map of words which you associate with hi-tech Japan. Include both English and Japanese words and set out your map like the one below. Next, compare it with a partner's. Then, working together, find the Japanese version of the English words you wrote. If you need help, refer to the vocabulary list for this unit on page 20 of the *Textbook*, or a dictionary, or ask your teacher.

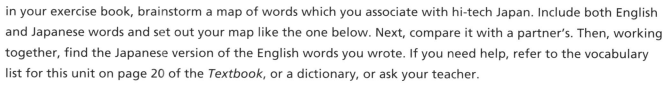

たんご   TB. P20

1

Match the Japanese word with its English equivalent.

ねだん	car navigation system		もの	apple
アニメ	internet		ほしいもの	blue
手ちょう	convenient, useful		ブルー（の）	thing
カーナビ	horrible		おこづかい	strawberry
いや（な）	silver		いちご	things you want
インターネット	price		もらいます	allowance, pocket money
べんり（な）	animation, cartoons		りんご	receive
シルバー（の）	organiser			

2 ✍

Complete the following Japanese words so that they belong to each given category AND have the correct number of characters. Then give the English meaning.

CATEGORY

A hi-tech product	___ デ ___ ___ ___	_____
A colour	___ ル ___ の	_____
A leisure activity/ sport	___ よ ___ ___	_____
A fruit	___ ___ か	_____
A style of music	___ ッ ___ ___	_____

> Create your own game using the vocabulary from page 20 of 「ほしいもの」. Test it on your friends!

> ⓘ Have you been using the hints mentioned in 「わたし」 to help you learn your kanji?
> Here are some other methods to help you remember new vocabulary. Choose one that suits you and try it. See what a difference it can make!
>
> - Try to make up stories that link new words with the words you already know.
>   E.g. すいじょうスキー
>   すい is from "swimming" (すいえい)
>   じょう is from "good at" (じょうず)
>   スキー is "snow skiing"
>   So, if you're good at swimming and snow skiing, water skiing will be easy!
>
> - Make small cards with a Japanese word on one side, and the English meaning plus the romaji reading of the Japanese word on the other. Ask a family member to test you by saying a word in English. Impress them by responding quickly with the Japanese equivalent. They can check your answer by reading the romaji.

かんじ TB. P21

3 ✍

Write the following words in hiragana.

ⓐ 中学校 ☐☐☐☐☐☐

ⓑ 買いもの ☐☐☐☐☐

ⓒ 電子 ☐☐☐

ⓓ 新しい ☐☐☐☐

ⓔ 番ごう ☐☐☐☐

> ⓘ When writing horizontally place the small や, ゆ, よ or つ in the bottom left corner of the square.

Practise writing these new kanji in the boxes provided.

中							
新							
買							
電							
方							
番							

- Write new words in Japanese on pieces of paper and stick them on the fridge. Don't open the door until you can say the English meaning of each new word!
- Draw a line down the centre of a piece of paper. In one column, write a Japanese word and in the other column, write the English meaning. Then cover one column at a time and check which words you know.

5

Use kanji to complete the sentences using the English hints. Add any necessary *okurigana*.

> *Okurigana* is hiragana added after kanji. For example, the *okurigana* for 行きました is きました and the *okurigana* for 行って is って.

_____ のおとうとは _____ です。
　my　　　　　　　a junior high school student

げん気な _____ です。_____ が _____ です。
　　　　　　boy　　　　　　　　　　　shopping　　　　　likes

_____ けいたい _____ がほしいです。
　　new　　　　　　　　　　　phone

ハイテク日本　　TB P 22-23

6

Practise writing and saying how something looks. Think about whether each adjective is an い or な adjective. Can you see the different pattern in the way they change?

	おいしい	おいしそう	(It) looks delicious
a	たのしい		
b	おもしろい		
c	いい		
d	べんり		
e	まじめ		

7

You will hear some people talking about what they want to do.

a) Listen, and write the number of the conversation next to the appropriate word.

b) Listen again, and this time write down in English what the thing they are talking about looks like.

(　　) 読みたいです。　_____

(　　) 買いたいです。　_____

(　　) 行きたいです。　_____

(　　) 食べたいです。　_____

第二課　二十

8 書 ? P32

Re-write these sentences in your exercise book to mean 'I want to …'. Take care with particles. When you have finished, compare your sentences with a partner.

a この新しいけいたい電話をつかいます。　　**c** けいたい電話で友だちと話します。

b ＤＶＤでアニメやえいがを見ます。　　**d** 土曜日に友だちとでかけます。

9 読

The following tasks are based on information about ハイテク日本 on page 22 of the *Textbook*.

a Read the introductory paragraph, then complete this sentence in English:

Hi-tech goods are popular with both children and adults because
_____.

b Beside each sentence write in Japanese the name of the hi-tech product to which it refers.

メールを書いて、おくれます。　＿＿＿＿＿＿＿＿＿＿＿＿＿＿

じ書のきのうがあります。　＿＿＿＿＿＿＿＿＿＿＿＿＿＿

しゃしんがとれます。　＿＿＿＿＿＿＿＿＿＿＿＿＿＿

えがとてもリアルです。　＿＿＿＿＿＿＿＿＿＿＿＿＿＿

ドライブにとてもべんりです。　＿＿＿＿＿＿＿＿＿＿＿＿＿＿

アニメが見られます。　＿＿＿＿＿＿＿＿＿＿＿＿＿＿

パーソナルインフォーメーションがインプットできます。　＿＿＿＿＿＿＿＿＿

c You are planning to buy souvenirs for your family and friends on your next trip to 日本. Read the information about the four hi-tech products, and then answer these questions in English.

1 For whom would you be most likely to buy the 電子手ちょう? Why?
_____

2 Would you buy a けいたい電話? For whom? Explain your answer.
_____

d Read the bottom paragraph and use the information to complete these sentences in English.

1 Japanese high school students _____.

2 Japanese mothers _____.

3 Japanese fathers _____.

10

ゆみ and けん are looking at the latest edition of a magazine which advertises hi-tech products.

a Listen to their conversations and decide which hi-tech product they are speaking about. Write the number of the conversation in the box beside the corresponding picture.

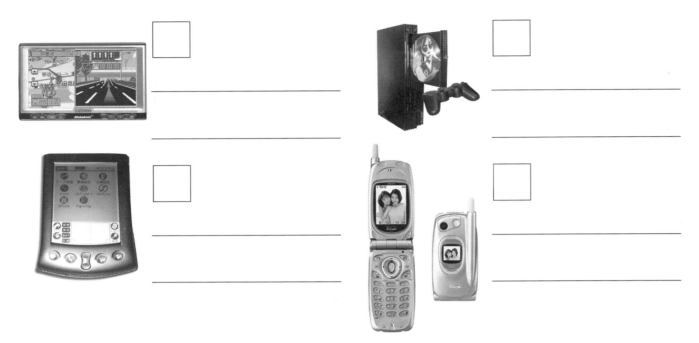

b Listen again. This time listen for the key words that give their opinions of each product. Write them in English in the space provided.

11

You have been invited to contribute a feature article about a new hi-tech product for the next edition of 「ほしいもの」. In your exercise book write a draft paragraph about 50 字 in length. When you have proofread your article and you are satisfied that there are no errors, write the final version on paper, or present it using Microsoft Word, Power Point, Publisher or similar software.

Option 1: Use the English hints below and the passages on page 22 of the *Textbook* as your models to write a paragraph about the digital movie camera shown.

- Looks hi-tech
- Not expensive
- Can take photos
- I want to use it
- Can make movies

Option 2: Create your own article about your favourite hi-tech item. Include a picture.

第二課　二十二

ピピピッ! TB. P24-25

12

Write the English meaning of the following sentences in your exercise book.

ⓐ 母はコーヒーよりこうちゃの方が好きです。

ⓑ 日本ではサッカーの方がテニスより人気があります。

ⓒ ぼくはカメラよりけいたい電話の方がほしいです。

ⓓ 私はすうがくよりかがくの方がとくいです。

13

You will hear some short conversations. As you listen, circle the correct alternatives in the following English sentences.

ⓐ けい子 prefers (lemonade, cola).

ⓑ (ひろし、こうた) is taller.

ⓒ えり thinks (German, French) is more difficult.

ⓓ A (bus, train) is more convenient to go to town.

14

In your exercise book, use the words given to form the question 'Which one?' (of two items). Then write an answer for each question. The first one has been done for you.

ⓐ いぬ、ねこ、好き   Q: いぬとねことどちらの方が好きですか。
　　　　　　　　　　　　A: ねこの方が好きです。

ⓑ テニス、すいえい、とくい

ⓒ ピザ、ハンバーガー、おいしい

ⓓ けいたい電話、インターネット、べんり

ⓔ 日本語、すうがく、やさしい

15

Part A

Look at the cartoon (ピピピッ！) on page 24 of the *Textbook*. Listen to the conversation and jot down any key words such as colours, opinions and features in the space provided. Then, complete the sentences below summarising what happens.

a At first, the boy prefers the _____ mobile phone.

b That phone is _____ and _____.

c Select the best alternative:

The girl thinks that 1 karaoke is more interesting than the TV phone.

2 The TV phone is more interesting than karaoke.

d The boy decides to buy the _____ mobile phone.

Part B

With a partner, role-play this cartoon for your class. See if you can make some changes to the colours and features of the phones and the opinions given.

16

Listen to えり and よし子 discussing clothes in a department store. As you listen, make notes in the space provided. Then, answer the questions in English.

a What is the problem with the black skirt?

_____
_____

b What sort of skirt does えり prefer?

_____
_____

c Which skirt does よし子 suggest?

_____
_____

d What does よし子 finally suggest?

_____
_____

17

けんご and his girlfriend, みち子, have decided to watch a movie at home tonight. They are at the video store.

PART A
Complete the following conversation by converting the English parts to Japanese.

けんご： 今ばん、ビデオを見ませんか。

みち子： _____
(That's good.)

けんご： サスペンスのえいがはどうですか。

みち子： _____
(Umm… I like action movies more than suspense movies.)

けんご： そうですか。じゃ、スパイダー・マンとロード・オブ・リングがあります。

みち子： _____
(Which is more interesting? スパイダー・マン or ロード・オブ・リング)

けんご： _____
(Umm… スパイダー・マン is more interesting. It looks good.)

みち子： いいですね。じゃ、スパイダー・マンを見ましょう。

PART B
Role-play the conversation above with a partner. Try to make some changes to the types and names of videos.

一番いい   TB. P 26-27

18

a Compare the following items. Write a question in Japanese for each set of illustrations and give your answer. Remember you are comparing **more than** two items. Think about what adjective is most appropriate.

チョコレート　　イチゴ　　バニラ

Q: _____
A: _____

Q: _____
A: _____

b Now, ask your friend the questions you wrote above and compare their answer with yours.

19

Complete the following sentences using 一番 and appropriate adjectives. The first one is done for you. Notice that it uses the particle は, for example, ふじ山 **は** 日本で一番高いです。 When you are just making a statement and not responding to a question, you should use は with the subject.

a ふじ山は日本で一番高いです。

b すうがくは _____ 。

c イアン・ソープは _____ 。

d バスケット・ボールは _____ 。

e 日本のハイテクグッズは _____ 。

20

Read the following statements and decide if each one is true (〇) or false (✘). Then design two of your own statements. Write them in your exercise book, before challenging your friends.

a せかいのタワーの中で東京タワーは一番高いです。　〇　✘

b やきゅうはオーストラリアで一番人気があります。　〇　✘

c カナダはせかいのくにの中で一番大きいです。　〇　✘

d いぬの中でチワワは一番小さいです。　〇　✘

21

Listen to ゆたか reading out loud to his class telling them the results of a class survey about TV programs. As you listen, try to pick out the following key points and write them in English in the space provided.

a) Three popular types of programs:

_____ _____ _____

b) The most popular type of program: _____

c) The most popular sports program: _____

d) The player liked by girls: _____

e) The player liked by boys: _____

22

a) Here is some information about a band.

- underline the Japanese for "the coolest"
- highlight the Japanese for "very popular"
- copy the Japanese for "trendy and cool" below

_____

- circle the Japanese for "very nice"
- underline the Japanese for "the newest"

b) Look at the information about the most fashionable drink.

- circle the Japanese for "most fashionable"
- Give the English for:

コーラとオレンジ・ジュースと生茶(なまちゃ)の中で、どれが一番おしゃれですか。

_____

_____

- highlight the sentence which tells what is most popular
- underline "it's more popular than cola"
- write a Japanese sentence saying what the price is

_____

23

What is the most fashionable snack, magazine, CD or computer game in your country at the moment? Write an article about 50 – 100 字 in length to describe **one** of the fashionable items in your country. You can write either on paper, or use Microsoft Word, Power Point, Publisher or similar software. A web search may help you find a suitable illustration, or you could photocopy a picture from a magazine.

Once you have decided what to write about, make a plan and write down the key features you will mention. Then, write the article including the title, your name and an illustration. Set out your article by following the typical plan and structure shown in the example below.

Example:

This is a typical plan, with key points and useful vocabulary.

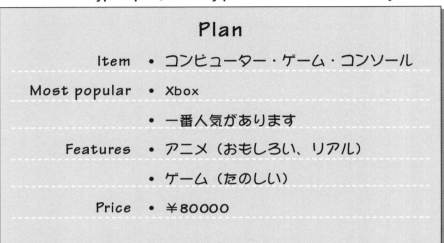

Plan

Item	• コンピューター・ゲーム・コンソール
Most popular	• Xbox
	• 一番人気があります
Features	• アニメ（おもしろい、リアル）
	• ゲーム（たのしい）
Price	• ￥80000

This shows the typical structure of an article.

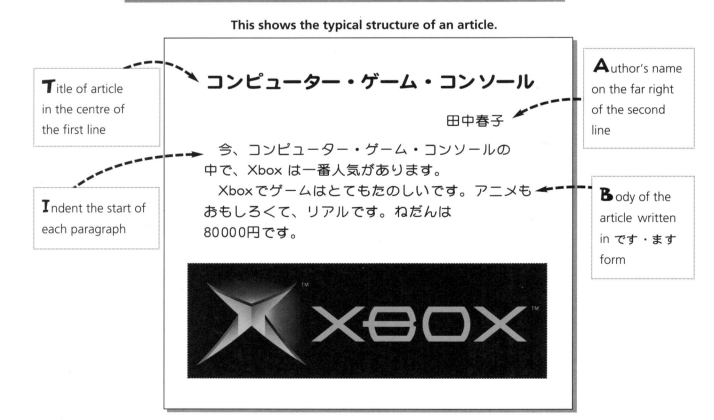

- **T**itle of article in the centre of the first line
- **A**uthor's name on the far right of the second line
- **I**ndent the start of each paragraph
- **B**ody of the article written in です・ます form

Article text:

コンピューター・ゲーム・コンソール

　　　　　　　　　　田中春子

　今、コンピューター・ゲーム・コンソールの中で、Xboxは一番人気があります。
　Xboxでゲームはとてもたのしいです。アニメもおもしろくて、リアルです。ねだんは80000円です。

とくしゅう

TB. P 28-29

24

Refer to the pie chart and graph on page 28 of the *Textbook*, and answer the following questions in English in your exercise book.

a What were the two questions asked in this survey?
b How many students were interviewed?
c How many students said they receive between ￥10 001 and ￥20 000?
d What is the most common amount of pocket money?
e What is the most common item purchased with pocket money?
f How many students responded that they use their allowance to buy sweets and drinks?

25

Read the とくしゅう page, おこづかいはいくらですか, on page 29 of the *Textbook*. Use the information to complete a summary of こうた's statement and/or さちか's statement.

a こうたくんは月に ＿＿＿＿ おこづかいをもらいます。食べものと ＿＿＿＿ に 4 000円つかいます。3 000円で ＿＿＿＿ や ＿＿＿＿ を買って、＿＿＿＿ を ビデオゲームにつかいます。eメールは月に ＿＿＿＿ です。こうたくんの ＿＿＿＿ は土曜日です。＿＿＿＿ や ＿＿＿＿ であそびたいです。 でも、高いです。だから、＿＿＿＿ ざっしとまんがを買いません。

b さちかさんは月に ＿＿＿＿ を ＿＿＿＿ 円もらいます。＿＿＿＿ に 12 000円かかります。＿＿＿＿ に10 000円、まんがに ＿＿＿＿ つかいます。 ＿＿＿＿ やカラオケボックスに5 000円はらいます。さちかさんはGlayが大好きです。 ＿＿＿＿ GlayのCDがはやく聞きたいです。

26

Listen to いちろう interview けい子 about her allowance. As you listen, note down the main points in the space provided. Then use the information to write answers to the questions in English.

- Before you listen, read the English questions. Try to guess what いちろう might ask, and what けい子 might reply.
- After you have finished, check to see that it all makes sense.

a) How much pocket money does けい子 get?

b) What does she buy with 6000 yen and why?

c) How much does she spend for snacks?

27

What are the top two items bought with pocket money in your class?

PART A

Prepare a survey sheet in your exercise book which includes Japanese for the question "What do you buy with your pocket money?". You should leave space for the responses of ten class mates. When you have prepared your survey sheet, conduct your interviews, in Japanese of course.

PART B

After the interviews, collate the data about the items which are purchased with pocket money. Prepare a column graph like that on page 28 of the *Textbook* to show the data, either on paper or using suitable computer software.

つかってみよう

28

The following graph shows the results of a survey in the newspaper about ほしいもの. You are preparing to talk about the survey results in class tomorrow. Write five sentences about the results in Japanese and practise reading the sentences aloud. Use the examples in the box to guide you.

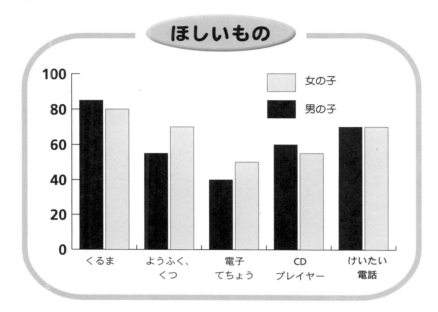

ＣＤプレイヤーは男の子に人気があります。
55パーセントの女の子のほしいものはＣＤプレイヤーです。
男の子は電子てちょうよりくるまの方がほしいです。

ⓐ _____
ⓑ _____
ⓒ _____
ⓓ _____
ⓔ _____

The following phrases may help you describe the results of the survey.

パーセント (percentage)　　一番　　～より～の方
人気があります。　　　　　ほしいです。

Option 1: Using Microsoft Word, Power Point, Publisher or similar software, prepare a six-page picture story book, with the title 「ほしいもの」. For each page, include a picture, some Japanese text and a recording of your own voice telling the story.

You can make all six pages yourself, or you can choose to use the following pages one and five as part of your story.

ほしいもの。

オートバイより、くるまの方が好きです。
買いたいです。でも...

Option 2: Create a jingle for a radio or television promotion of a new soft drink, snack food or electronic gadget. You might like to write the words to accompany a well-known tune, or alternatively, try to compose your own music and words. Aim for about a 30 second jingle that incorporates a variety of interesting language which will appeal to teenagers.

Option 3: Imagine that you have won a $10,000 prize in the lottery! Write an imaginative story, about 150 字 long, in which you detail how you will use your prize money.

lottery	たからくじ
win	かちます
receive	もらいます
give	あげます

おしゃべり   TB. P34-35

30 読書

Find the plain form of these verbs hidden horizontally and vertically in the puzzle. Five hiragana will remain. Use them to answer the question.

つかいます	ねます	およいでいます
もらいます	おきます	のんでいます
あそびます	でかけます	うたっています
つくります	できます	まっています
あるきます	きます (wear)	しています
します	きます (come)	

う	た	っ	て	い	る	か	で
お	よ	い	で	い	る	の	き
い	で	か	け	る	て	ん	る
ね	る	る	あ	そ	ぶ	で	つ
く	る	の	お	き	る	い	か
す	き	る	も	ら	う	る	う
る	あ	る	く	し	て	い	る
ま	っ	て	い	る	つ	く	る

Question: 何してるの？

Answer: _____

31 聞

Listen to a telephone conversation between けん and じろう. Answer the following questions as indicated.

a Tick the picture which shows what けん is doing now.

b Tick the picture which shows what じろう is doing now.

c Answer the following questions in full English sentences.

1. Where is じろう going tomorrow? _____

2. What does he want to do there? _____

3. What time do the boys decide to meet tomorrow? _____

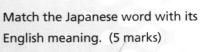

When you have completed the 「ほしいもの」unit, try this quiz to see how well you have mastered the key vocabulary, kanji and grammar.

A
Match the Japanese word with its English meaning. (5 marks)

もらいます	convenient
新しい	new
おこづかい	receive
ねだん	allowance
べんり	price

B
Write the underlined words in hiragana in the space provided. Include *okurigana* if needed. (11 marks)

1 まい日、新聞（　　　　　）を買います（　　　　　）。

2 ぼくは男の子（　　　　　）の中学校（　　　　　）に 行って（　　　　　）います。

3 今、電子手ちょう（　　　　　）が一番（　　　　　） 新しい（　　　　　）です。

4 よく、友だち（　　　　　）と電話（　　　　　）で話します（　　　　　）。

C
Change the words into the form indicated in brackets. (4 marks)

1　書きます (want to...)
_____

3　やさしい (it looks...)
_____

2　会います (want to...)
_____

4　べんり (it looks...)
_____

D
Write the following sentences in Japanese. (8 marks)

1　That movie looks good. Let's see it tomorrow.
_____

2　I want to play tennis with my father on Saturday.
_____

3　Which do you prefer, classical music or rock music?
_____

4　That video game is the most expensive.
_____

E
Fill in the blanks with particles. (7 marks)

1　おこづかい（　　）ほしいです。

2　おとうとはべんきょうよりスポーツの方（　　）好きです。

3　きみ子さんは月（　　）20 000円、おこづかい（　　）もらいます。

4　まい日おひるごはん（　　）5ドルつかいます。

5　Glay（　　）CD（　　）聞きたいです。

Check your answers against those on page 101. Give yourself a score and read the assessment at the bottom of the page.

第二課　三十四

34

しゅうまつ

As you look at the cover of the third 'magazine' on page 37 of the *Textbook*, discuss the following points.

- The title of this magazine is 「しゅうまつ」, which means 'weekend'. Which kanji do you think might be しゅうまつ?
- Look at the Japanese people on the cover. Where are they? How do you think they spend their weekends? Be prepared to share your ideas with the class.
- What is the とくしゅう for this magazine? What does it mean in English?
- Name two activities, written in katakana, which you expect to find in 「しゅうまつ」.

たんご　　　　　　　　　　　　　TB. P38

Complete the following sentences with an appropriate verb from the box below. When you have finished, one verb will remain. Use it to write a sentence of your own.

> でかけます　　とまりました　　かえりました　　のみたいです
> もっています　　すいません　　ぶらぶらします　　たのしみます

a) 私はたばこを _____。

b) しゅうまつにスポーツを _____。

c) きのう、よるおそくうちに _____。

d) 日本できれいなホテルに _____。

e) のどがかわきました。水が _____。

f) けい子さんはすてきなとけいを _____。

g) 土曜日のよる、友だちと _____。

h) _____。

 You will find that there is an emphasis on verbs in this unit. Choose one of the learning hints from Unit 2 and use it to memorise all the new verbs in this unit.

2

Your class is going to play a word game called 「えであてよう」, in which you take turns to draw a picture representing a Japanese word. You may not write words or Japanese characters in your pictures. Look at the example on the right.

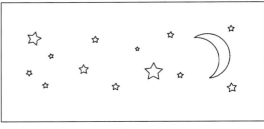

よる

Game Preparation

Try drawing pictures for the following words.

私たち	まんがきっさ	せかい

Game

To play the game, form small groups of about three or four people. Take turns drawing a picture for any words in the vocabulary list on page 38 of the *Textbook*. See how quickly the members of your group can guess the word. After you have practised, compete against other groups in your class.

Try drawing a sequence of pictures to represent a whole sentence. Can your team-mates guess the complete Japanese sentence?

しゅうまつにうみでサイクリングをします。

第三課　三十六

かんじ

TB. P39

3

Practise writing these new kanji in the boxes provided.

毎							
週							
飲							
帰							
休							

Using Power Point, create your own electronic kanji flashcards that automatically flip over.
First, design the look of your basic slide. You will need just one textbox on each slide.
From the **Format** menu, select **Font**. A good size for the font is 200 points. Type this number directly into the **Size** box.
From the **Slide Show** menu, select **Slide Transition**. Set your slides to **Advance automatically after one second**. When you have finished, click on **Apply to all**.

For each kanji, you will need to create three slides. On the first slide type in the kanji, on the second type in the kanji reading, and on the third type the meaning in English.

Note: For PC users, MS Office 2000 (or higher) with Windows 2000 (or higher) is required to write Japanese script in Power Point. The Japanese language option must also be enabled. For Mac users, MS Office 2000 (or higher) with Japanese Language Kit is the minimum.

4 (聞)

Listen to some sentences in Japanese. Circle the correct kanji from the options given in the brackets.

a) ｛ 今年、今月、今日 ｝ トムさんとあそびました。

b) いもうとは ｛ 今年、今月、今日 ｝ ｛ 中学校、中学生、高校生 ｝ です。

c) ｛ 今週、毎日、毎週 ｝ ｛ 水曜日、金曜日、木曜日 ｝ に テニスをします。

d) 父は ｛ 毎月、毎年、毎日 ｝ さんぽをします。

> ! You will find this easier if you read the options first and think about the meaning of each kanji.

5 (書)

a) Combine two (or more) kanji characters from the box to make a word. Characters may be used more than once. Aim to write at least eight words in the space below. When you are finished, check to see how well you scored.

毎	高	今	一	書
電	週	学	読	子
話	生	番	年	校

_____

_____

_____

_____

何てんでしたか。

more than 8:	たいへんよくできました。おめでとう。
7 or 8 words:	よくできました。
5 or 6:	まあまあです。
less than 5:	もっと、がんばってください。 Time to look at the hints in Unit 1 and 2 again and try a new trick for memorising kanji.

b) Show that you understand the meaning of the words you have written by using five in separate Japanese sentences. Here is an example.

｛毎週｝: 毎週、友だちとまちに行って、ぶらぶらします。

1 _____

2 _____

3 _____

4 _____

5 _____

第三課　三十八

今月のクイズ   TB. P40-41

6

Complete the following table. Check your answers using the Glossary on pages 106 and 107 of the *Textbook*.

英語	〜ます form	〜て form
	すいます	
have/hold		
		帰って
write		
	およぎます	
		飲んで
	でかけます	
sleep		
wake up		
		して
come		

7

Here is the survey from 「しゅうまつ」. It looks fun! Give it a go!

- パーティーに行ってもいいですか。
  - はい、いいです。
  - いいえ、だめです。
- アルコールを飲んでもいいですか。
  - はい、いいです。
  - いいえ、だめです。
- たばこをすってもいいですか。
  - はい、いいです。
  - いいえ、だめです。
- よるおそくうちに帰ってもいいですか。
  - はい、いいです。
  - いいえ、だめです。
- 友だちとでかけてもいいですか。
  - はい、いいです。
  - いいえ、だめです。
- デートをしてもいいですか。
  - はい、いいです。
  - いいえ、だめです。

> When you have finished, compare your answers with someone you don't know very well and find out what they are allowed to do at the weekend.

8

a Listen to まさる ask his mother for permission to do various things. Circle his mother's responses.

1	allowed	not allowed
2	allowed	not allowed
3	allowed	not allowed
4	allowed	not allowed
5	allowed	not allowed
6	allowed	not allowed

Key points
1 _____
2 _____
3 _____
4 _____
5 _____
6 _____

b Listen again, noting the key point of each of まさる's questions in English. Then, write some sentences in Japanese explaining what まさる is allowed to do this weekend.

_____
_____
_____

9

Ben will soon be spending three weeks on exchange with the 山田さんのかぞく. He has decided in his next letter, to ask a few questions about rules in the 山田さんのうち. In preparation for that next letter, show Ben how to ask permission to do the activities pictured. The first one is completed as an example.

一 　ビデオゲームをしてもいいですか。

四 　_____

二 　_____

五 　_____

三 　_____

六 　_____

第三課　四十

えいがかんのきそく TB. P42-43

10

Brainstorm with a partner places where you are <u>not allowed</u> to do the following things. Write the names of the places in Japanese beside each rule. Try to use a different place for each rule.

ⓐ しゃしんをとってはいけません。＿＿＿＿＿＿＿＿＿＿＿＿＿＿

ⓑ おかしを食べてはいけません。＿＿＿＿＿＿＿＿＿＿＿＿＿＿

ⓒ たばこをすってはいけません。＿＿＿＿＿＿＿＿＿＿＿＿＿＿

ⓓ けいたい電話をつかってはいけません。＿＿＿＿＿＿＿＿＿＿＿

ⓔ 大きいこえで話してはいけません。＿＿＿＿＿＿＿＿＿＿＿＿

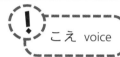
こえ　voice

11

Re-write the following sentences to mean that the activities are not allowed. The first one is done for you.

ⓐ へやの中であそびます。　→　へやの中であそんではいけません。

ⓑ このしゃしんを先生に見せます。
＿＿＿＿＿＿＿＿＿＿＿＿＿＿＿＿＿＿＿＿＿＿＿＿＿＿

ⓒ たけしくんとでかけます。
＿＿＿＿＿＿＿＿＿＿＿＿＿＿＿＿＿＿＿＿＿＿＿＿＿＿

ⓓ ここでおよぎます。
＿＿＿＿＿＿＿＿＿＿＿＿＿＿＿＿＿＿＿＿＿＿＿＿＿＿

ⓔ あした、パーティーに行きます。
＿＿＿＿＿＿＿＿＿＿＿＿＿＿＿＿＿＿＿＿＿＿＿＿＿＿

ⓕ よるおそくCDを聞きます。
＿＿＿＿＿＿＿＿＿＿＿＿＿＿＿＿＿＿＿＿＿＿＿＿＿＿

12

These children are asking their parents for permission to do various activities. Today, the children are not allowed to do what they ask. Complete the speech bubbles with Japanese questions and responses.

13

Read えいがかんのきそく on page 42 of the *Textbook* and complete the following tasks in English.

a) Circle the correct alternatives:

Paul is an { Australian   American   African } studying in { Osaka   Tokyo   Kyoto }.

b) What sort of information does Paul want?

_____

c) How does the author of the response describe the rules in Japanese cinemas?

_____

d) What four things are not allowed at the 新大阪えいがかん?

_____

_____

_____

_____

14

Listen to a teacher explaining to his class the rules for the class excursion to an amusement park （ゆうえんち）. As you listen, make notes about the rules and then write a summary in English.

Amusement Park Excursion Rules

Allowed to:
-
-
-

Not allowed to:
-
-
-

15

There are many rules of etiquette in Japan and Australia. Read the following text about some rules in Japan and Australia and complete the table in English.

日本にもオーストラリアにもいろいろなきそくがあります。日本では、たいていうちの中でくつをはいてはいけません。げんかんでくつをぬいで、スリッパをはきます。でも、オーストラリアでは、うちの中でくつをはいてもいいです。

オーストラリアでたばこのきそくはきびしいです。でも、日本ではレストランやビルの中でたばこをすってもいいです。

オーストラリアでは１８さいからくるまのうんてんができます。たばこをすって、ワインやビールを飲んでもいいです。

日本でははたちまでうんてんしてはいけません。そして、たばこもアルコールもだめです。

たんご:
- たいてい　usually
- げんかん　the entrance hall
- ぬぐ　to take off
- うんてん　driving

	Japan	Australia
Shoes		
Smoking		
Alcohol		
Driving		

せかいの高校生にインタビュー... TB. P44-45

16   P50; P106-109

a Complete the following table.

	～ます form	～て form	～たり form
Group 1	うたいます		
	休みます		
	あるきます		
	とまります		
	話します		
Group 2	食べます		
	見ます		
Irreg.	きます (come)		
	ぶらぶらします		

b Prepare for a class game of Bingo by writing each of the verbs above in ～たり form into the following grid. Your teacher will then call out the verbs at random. Locate each verb in the grid as you hear it and put a cross through it. When you have three crossed out in a row (in any direction) call out ビンゴ！

17   P50

In your exercise book, re-write the following sentences in the negative.

a きのう、テレビを見ました。

b 土曜日のごご、テニスのれんしゅうを休みました。

c 金曜日のよる、パーティーに行きました。

d 私は週まつにべんきょうしたり、としょかんに行ったりします。

チャレンジ！

Write a sentence of your own and challenge a friend to re-write it in the negative.

18

Choose an appropriate particle from the box to complete the sentences.

a. きのう、よるおそくうち（　）帰りました。

b. 週まつにデート（　）してもいいです。

c. レストラン（　）たばこをすってはいけません。

d. 友だちとえいが（　）見たいです。

e. ぼくはいつもガールフレンド（　）えみちゃん（　）でかけます。

```
を    に    が
で    の    と
```

19

Write sentences using all the given words and the 〜たり〜たり pattern. When you have finished, ask a friend to check your sentences, particularly your particles and verbs. The first one is done for you.

a. 母、週まつ、買いもの、ざっし

母は週まつに買いものをしたり、ざっしを読んだりします。

b. 土曜日、友だち、えいが、ゲーム・センター

_____

c. パーティー、ピザ、うた

_____

d. なつ休み、うみ、およぎます、サーフィン

_____

e. 日曜日、ボーイフレンド、テレビ、聞きます

_____

20

You will hear six international high school students talk about their typical weekend activities. As you listen, fill in the missing activities for each person in this English summary.

Anna	Ski jumps, _____
Chisato	Window shopping, _____, _____
John	_____, watch movies
Yan	_____, talk with friends at cafes
Emmanuel	Television soccer games, _____
Sophie	Swimming at the beach, _____

21

けんじ is interviewing four of his Japanese friends about how they spend their weekends.

a As you listen, make notes in English or Japanese on the following guided note-taking sheet.

名前	週まつに何をしますか。
1 みち子	
2 えり子	
3 こうた	
4 ひろゆき	

b Based on the information you have noted down, in your exercise book write one sentence in Japanese about each of けんじ's friends, including their name and what they do on the weekend.

22

Read Kelly's description of her typical weekend and answer the questions in English in your exercise book.

　　私は土曜日にパンやであさ九時からごご二時までアルバイトをしています。私はパンやドーナツやマフィンをつくります。おひるにみせのおいしいパンを食べてもいいです。私はこのアルバイトが好きです。

　　アルバイトのあとで、たいてい友だちに電話をかけたり、まちに買いものに行ったりします。時々、パーティーに行きます。

　　日曜日には、あさ十時におきます。そして、いぬのハッピーとさんぽをします。かぞくとテニスをしたり、フットボールを見たりします。よる、でかけてはいけません。うちでしゅくだいをします。

　　週まつはとてもいそがしいです。でも、たのしいです。

> パンや bakery

a When and for how long does Kelly work at the bakery?

b What is Kelly's job at the bakery?

c What advantage does Kelly have in working at the bakery?

d Besides her part-time job, what does Kelly do on Saturday?

e What time does Kelly get up on Sunday?

f What does Kelly do with her family on Sunday?

g Why do you think Kelly is not allowed to go out on Sunday night?

とくしゅう   TB. P46-47

23

Read about 山川こうたろう's weekend on page 46 of the *Textbook*. Answer these questions in English.

a) こうたろう lists three strict rules at his school. What are they?

- _____
- _____
- _____

ぼくのうちにとまりませんか。

b) What are five activities こうたろう does at weekends and on holidays?

- _____   • _____
- _____   • _____
- _____

c) If you went to stay with こうたろう:

1. how would you feel studying at his school? Why?
   _____

2. how much leisure time would you spend with こうたろう? Why?
   _____
   _____

24

Read what としき has to say on page 47 of the *Textbook* and complete the following English version of his story.

としき is currently at a school in Brisbane studying _____. He and his friends are all _____ years of age. They are very busy from _____ to _____. Every day, they go to school and then _____ and _____. At the weekend they don't _____. Often they go to clubs on Saturday. At the club they _____ and _____. としき really likes Australia. In Australia, 18 year-olds are allowed to _____ and _____. In Japan, however, until you are twenty, you are not allowed to _____, _____ or _____.

25

ⓐ 田中あき子 introduces herself and talks about her weekend. Listen carefully making notes on the following guided note-taking sheet in English or Japanese. Try to pick out the key points just from listening, before looking at the details of the text on page 46 of the *Textbook*.

```
Akiko's boyfriend
_____

_____

_____

Things Akiko does every weekend
_____

_____

_____

Rule about weekend dates
_____

_____

_____
```

ⓑ It is Monday morning. Imagine the conversation that might take place between あき子 and her friend, まり子. Using details from your guided note-taking sheet, complete the following conversation.

あき子： まり子さん、週まつはどうでしたか。

まり子： よかったです。えいがを見たり、かぞくとレストランに行ったりしました。あき子さんは？

あき子： ボーイフレンドの _____ と、こうえんに行きました。そして、ぶらぶらしたり、_____。

まり子： いいですね。土曜日のよる、でかけましたか。

あき子： はい、_____
_____

まり子： そうですか。何時に帰りましたか。

あき子： _____

つかってみよう

26

Imagine you are going to visit your sister school in Japan where you will be staying with まもる's family for two weeks. Because you want to know about まもる and his family you decide to phone Japan.

ⓐ Here is the script of part of a possible phone conversation between you and まもる. Read it and answer the questions below in English.

まもる：	ぼくは 15さいで、スポーツがすきです。
あなた：	まもるくんのかぞくは何人ですか。
まもる：	四人です。父と母とあねがいます。あねは高校三年生です。
あなた：	おねえさんはどんな人ですか。
まもる：	あねはあかるくて、じょうだんが好きです。英語が話せます。りょうりもとくいです。
あなた：	おねえさんはおもしろそうな人ですね。まもるくんも英語が話せますか。
まもる：	いいえ。ぼくは英語よりすうがくの方がとくいです。
あなた：	そうですか。週まつに何をしますか。
まもる：	友だちと買いものに行ったり、えいがを見たりします。日曜日にやきゅうをします。やきゅうが一番好きです。
あなた：	まもるくんは週まつにパーティーやまんがきっさに行ってもいいですか。
まもる：	はい。でもパーティーでビールを飲んだり、たばこをすったりしてはいけません。そして、おそくうちに帰ってはいけません。だから、ぼくはいつも十時までに帰ります。
あなた：	そうですか。日本でハイテクグッズが買いたいです。
まもる：	日本の電子手ちょうはいいですよ。インターネットができて、じしょのきのうがあります。
あなた：	べんりそうですね。でも高そうですね。
まもる：	ええ、でも、やすいみせがあります。週まつにいっしょに行きましょう。
あなた：	ああ、いいですね。たのしみです。

1 Describe まもる's sister. _____

2 What subject is まもる good at? _____

3 How does まもる spend his weekends? _____
_____

4 What is まもる not allowed to do at a party? _____

5 What does まもる recommend you buy in Japan and why? _____
_____

ⓑ Your school magazine is profiling the host families of the students who are going to Japan. You are to write an article about まもる and his family. Refer to the information provided in the phone conversation and write an article in your exercise book about 200 字 in length. Refer back to page 28 of this *Workbook* to see an example of how to lay out your article.

27

けい子 has sent your family the following e-mail. Read it carefully and underline her questions. Then, plan, draft and write a reply to her e-mail in Japanese in your exercise book or on your computer.

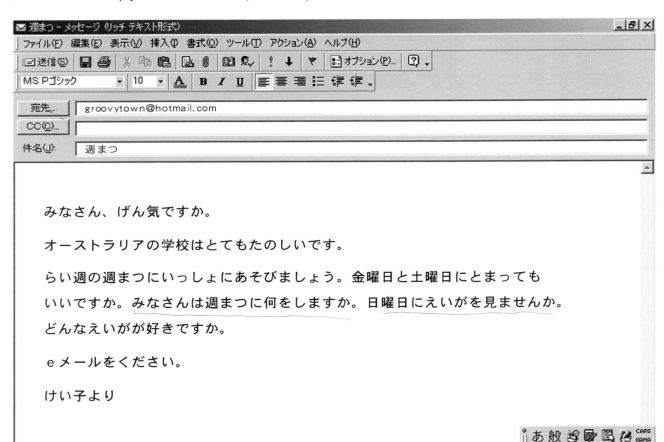

おしゃべり   TB. P 51-52

28

Re-write the following verbs, adjectives and nouns in the plain form past tense.

a) 見る _____   b) 飲む _____

c) 聞く _____   d) とまる _____

e) でかける _____   f) くる _____

g) する _____   h) 高い _____

i) べんりだ _____   j) いい天気だ _____

Read かおり and まさき's text messages to answer the questions.

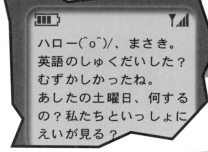
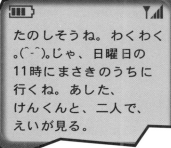

a Underline how かおり asks whether まさき finished his English homework.

b Circle かおり's invitation to see a movie together.

c Highlight how まさき declines かおり's invitation.

d Write out how まさき suggests another day and activity.

_____

e Underline the sentence in which かおり summarises the time and place she will go to meet まさき.

Tom and his friend, Tina, both study Japanese. They will spend some time together at the weekend. With a partner, take the roles of Tom and Tina and write a text message 'conversation' in Japanese casual speech style following these English suggestions. (The example in question 29 will be helpful.)

Tom: Says hello and asks about Tina's Japanese homework. He invites Tina to go to the city on Friday night.

Tina: Says she wants to go, but she practises piano on Friday night. She suggests they go for a walk on Sunday afternoon.

Tom: Agrees. He'll go to Tina's house at 12.00.

Tina: Confirms 12.00. Says good-bye.

クイズ!

When you have completed the 「週まつ」 unit, try this quiz to see how well you have mastered the key vocabulary, kanji and grammar.

A Write the matching English word. (4 marks)
1. たのしみます _____
2. とまります _____
3. もちます _____
4. きそく _____

B Write the matching Japanese word. (4 marks)
1. late 、 _____
2. everyday _____
3. night _____
4. world _____

C Read the following sentences, then use the *furigana* hints to write in the missing kanji. (7 marks)
1. じゅうぎょう（ ちゅう ）（ た ）べたり（ の ）んだりしてはだめです。
2. （ まいしゅう ）パーティーに行きます。でも、10時に（ かえ ）ります。
3. （ ことし ）ふゆ（ やす ）みに、かぞくといっしょにハワイに行きます。

D Convert the following sentences into Japanese. (10 marks)
1. You are allowed to play basketball. _____
2. You are not allowed to run. _____
3. May I use your computer? _____
4. Last weekend, I didn't do homework. _____
5. In the winter holidays, I do things like going skiing and reading books.
_____

E Combine each set of short sentences using the 〜たり〜たり form. (10 marks)
1. パーティーで（うたをうたいました。ＣＤを聞きました。）
_____
2. 週まつに（サイクリングをしました。えいがを見ました。）
_____
3. ひる休みに（バスケットボールをします。友だちと話します。）
_____
4. 日本で（しんかんせんにのります。ペンフレンドに会います。）
_____
5. 学校に（あるいて行きます。バスで行きます。）
_____

Check your answers against the solutions on page 101. Give yourself a score and read the assessment at the bottom of the page.

あるこう広島

Look at the cover of 「あるこう広島」 on page 53 of the *Textbook* and answer the following questions.

- This 'magazine' is part of a series of ガイド. What do you think is the special focus of this series?
- あるこう is the plain form for あるきましょう. How would you translate the title of this 'magazine' in English?
- Look at the images on page 53. Guess the name of the castle at the top. Work out the significance of the building on the right. Do you know what are hanging on the statue on the left? What does it look like they are cooking in the bottom picture?

たんご　　　　　　　　　　TB. P54

1

Using the ヒント！ find the Japanese words hidden horizontally or vertically in this puzzle. Four hiragana will remain. Use them to answer the question below.

そ	う	す	る	と	み	っ	つ	め
は	え	い	が	か	ん	か	ど	こ
し	ゆ	う	び	ん	き	ょ	く	う
ま	が	り	ま	す	こ	が	っ	え
し	ひ	と	つ	め	の	み	せ	ん
ん	ひ	あ	い	だ	へ	も	つ	ぎ
ご	ろ	ほ	ん	や	ん	う	ぎ	ん
う	い	ひ	だ	り	こ	み	ち	こ
み	ぎ	こ	う	さ	て	ん	う	う

ヒント！

post office	bank	bookshop	intersection
traffic lights	bridge	road	wide
right	left	cinema	already
turn	next	between	shop
around here	park	first	third
corner	then (after doing that)		

Q: 友だちはどこにいますか。

A: ＿＿＿＿＿＿＿＿＿＿＿＿＿＿＿＿ にいます。

2 Label the following picture in Japanese, using the hints provided.

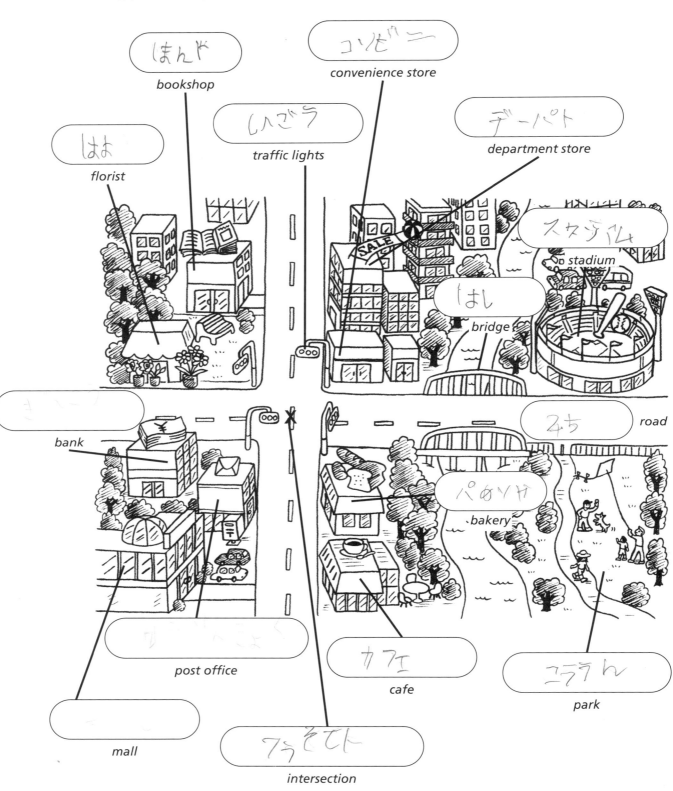

かんじ   TB. P55

3 書

Practise writing these new kanji in the boxes provided.

| 広 | 左 | 右 | 近 | 後 | 間 |

4 読

Look at each pair of kanji. Circle the kanji that has the greater number of strokes. When you have finished, compare your answers with a classmate.

a) 右 友   b) 左 行   c) 広 休
d) 近 会   e) 後 間   f) 食 高

5

Write the appropriate kanji and *okurigana* in the boxes, using the *furigana* above the boxes as a guide.

わたし　　　　　　　　　　ちかい　　　　　　　　　　　　ひろい
[　]のうちは、えきから[　][　]です。えきの[　][　]みちをまっすぐ

いって　　　　　　ひとつめ　　　　　　　ひだり
[　][　]、[　][　]のかどを[　]にまがります。そうすると、

がっこう　　　　　　　　　　　　　　　　がっこう　　　　うしろ
[　][　]があります。うちはその[　][　]の[　][　]にあります。

へいわモール　　　　　TB. P 56-57

6

What does this shopper want to know? Solve the puzzle, using hiragana, to find out. Then write his question in the empty speech bubble.

1　はなやは ＿＿＿ にありますか。
2　はなやはデパートと本や ＿＿＿ 間に
　　あります。
3　＿＿＿ モールにはみせがたくさんあります。
4　intersection
5　ATMはデパートの中 ＿＿＿ あります。
6　パンや ＿＿＿ どこですか。
7　inside
8　bookshop
9　ゆうびんきょく ＿＿＿ どこにありますか。
10　between
11　next to
12　in front
13　Excuse me …
14　コンビニはどこです ＿＿＿ 。

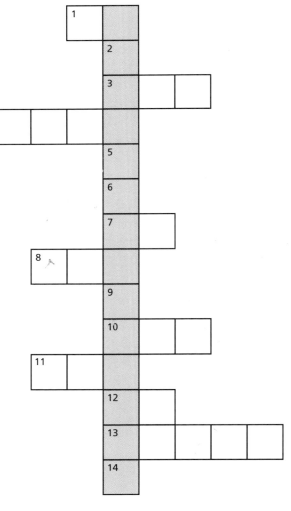

第四課　五十六

7

Look at this small shopping centre. Then fill the blanks in the sentences using appropriate words from the list given. Each word is to be used only once.

a) はなやはコンビニの ＿＿＿＿＿＿ にあります。

b) トイレはコンビニの ＿＿＿＿＿＿ です。

c) ATMはぎんこうの ＿＿＿＿＿＿ です。

d) カフェは ＿＿＿＿＿＿ と ＿＿＿＿＿＿ の ＿＿＿＿＿＿ にあります。

e) ゆうびんきょくは ＿＿＿＿＿＿ のとなりにあります。

間　前　となり
本や　はなや
後ろ　パンや

8

A new guide has started working at the information desk of へいわモール. As you listen to her responses, use this map and decide if her responses are correct. Circle either まる (correct) or ばつ (incorrect).

a) まる　ばつ
b) まる　ばつ
c) まる　ばつ
d) まる　ばつ
e) まる　ばつ

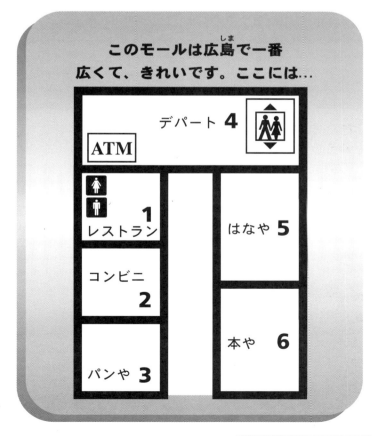

9

(a) Re-arrange the following words and sentences to create a likely conversation between a shopper and a guide at the へいわモール information desk. Write out your version of the conversation below.

- すみません、
- ありがとうございました。
- コンビニですか。
- いいえ、レストランとパンやの間にあります。
- ああ、わかりました。
- レストランと本やの間ですか。
- このへんにコンビニはありますか。
- コンビニはレストランとパンやの間です。
- おべんとうとジュースが買いたいです。

_____
_____
_____
_____
_____
_____

(b) Work with a partner to act out the conversation which you create in (a).

Or

Create your own conversation between a shopper and a guide at the information desk of your local mall. Act it out with a partner.

10

(a) You and your friend are going to work as ガイド at the へいわモール during the holidays. You have a fairly good knowledge of the lay-out of the mall, but it's time to test yourselves. Working separately, prepare five questions in Japanese asking for directions within the mall. Write them in your exercise book. Be sure to vary your questions so that your friend will get lots of practice.

(b) Work with your friend and ask each other your prepared questions. Check your answers carefully.

平和記念こうえん

TB. P58-59

11

Listen to のり子 give directions to the post office. Number each picture in the order you hear the directions. Then complete the final sentence in English.

( )   ( )   ( )   ( )

"The post office is next to the _____."

12

のぼる is an exchange student, staying with your family. He wants to go to the bank to get some money, before going to the department store to buy some おみやげ for his family. He asked you for directions. Refer to the map on page 59 of the *Textbook* to complete the tasks below.

a) In your exercise book write the directions from the school to the bank, and from the bank to the department store.

b) Read your directions to a partner who will follow them on the map to test the accuracy of what you have written.

 Here are some things to say to help you maintain the flow of your Japanese conversations.

To show your partner that you are interested and understand what is being said, try to use あいづち such as:

ああ、そうですか。	Is that so?
そうですね。	I agree.
いいですね。	That's good.
わかりました。	I understand.

When you are having difficulties following the conversation, try to use these:

すみません、もういちどいってください。
Please say that again.

すみません、ゆっくり話してください。
Please speak slowly.

すみません、ちょっとわかりません。
Sorry, I don't understand.

〜のいみは何ですか。
What does ____ mean?

〜は英語で何ですか。
What is ____ in English?

13

Look at the map of 平和記念こうえん (へいわきねん) on page 58 of the *Textbook* and read the conversation between the students and the man in uniform. Complete the following tasks.

a On the map, trace the path to be taken by the students.

b Write two ways to ask for directions to げんばくドーム in Japanese.

_____

_____

14

PART A

Look at 平和記念こうえん (へいわきねん) on page 58 of the *Textbook* and discuss the following questions.

a Find the sentence, 平和記念こうえんは広島(しま)で一番ゆうめいなこうえんです. What does this sentence mean?

b 英語で話してください。

1 Why do you think the Peace Memorial Park is so famous?

2 Why do you think the A-bomb Memorial Dome is in the Peace Memorial Park?

PART B

英語で…
Working in groups, do some research about 平和記念こうえん (へいわきねん) in 広島(しま), and present your findings to the class. Each member of the group is to do a 2–3 minute oral presentation in English about a different aspect of 平和記念こうえん (へいわきねん). The presentation is to be accompanied by either a Power Point presentation, a poster, or a collage to illustrate your key points.

Suggestions to get your research started:

- Use your library; ask your librarian
- Search the web – as well as the website given in the *Textbook*, (http://www.csi.ad.jp/ABOMB/index.html), check out the official homepage for the 広島(しま)平和記念(へいわきねん)こうえん, (http://www.pcf.city.hiroshima.jp/). There are lots of other sites too.

Questions to help your group decide what aspects of 平和記念 (へいわきねん) こうえん to talk about:

- What can you find in 平和記念 (へいわきねん) こうえん?
- What is the significance of these landmarks?
- What annual events are held?
- What would you be most interested in seeing and why?
- When/why were the park and buildings established?

第四課 六十

広島であそびましょう！ TB. P60-61

15

Read the conversation at the top of page 61 of the *Textbook*. Trace the path followed by the two people talking in the picture on the following map.

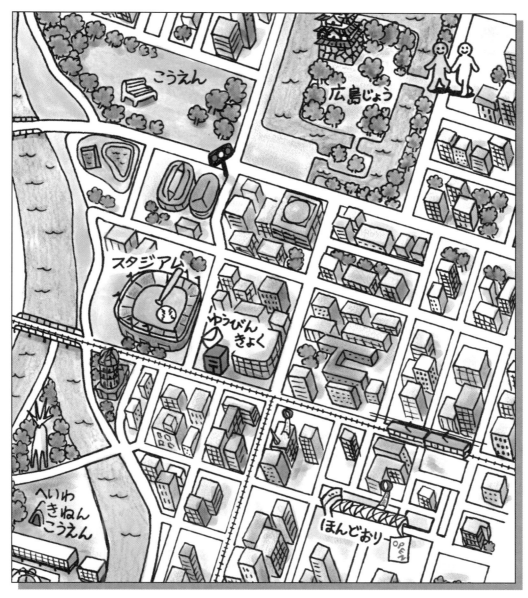

16

Looking at the map above, work with a partner to practise asking for and giving directions. Practise both roles.

a) You are at the gates of 広島じょう.

　Person A: Ask for directions to the post office.

　Person B: Give directions to the post office.

b) You are in front of the post office.

　Person A: Ask where ほんどおり is.

　Person B: Give directions to ほんどおり.

17

Listen to the conversation between よう子 and まさお and answer the following questions in English. Before you start, read the questions carefully. As you listen, make notes in the space provided.

a What does よう子 think of まさお's bag?
_____

b Why is まさお pleased with his bag?
_____

c On the map, mark the shop where まさお bought his bag.

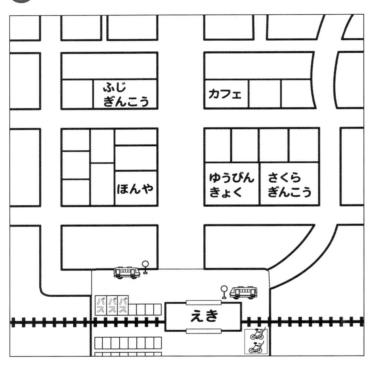

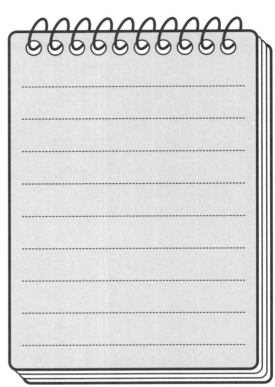

18   P65

Fill in each blank with an appropriate particle from the box. Particles may be used more than once.

| に | の | を | と |

　ぼくのうちはいろいろなみせやえきに近いです。コンビニはうちの前（　　）みち（　　）まっすぐ行って、一つ目（　　）かど（　　）左にまがります。そうすると、右がわ（　　）あります。ぎんこう（　　）となりです。ＫＦＣはコンビニ（　　）えいがかん（　　）間にあります。

第四課　六十二

とくしゅう

TB. P62-63

19

Imagine that you are living with a host family in Tokyo. Your friend, まさる, is a big fan of the Yokohama Bay Stars. You are going to meet him in Hiroshima to see the big baseball match between the Hiroshima Carp and the Bay Stars. In preparation for your trip to Hiroshima, you read a copy of the ベイ・スターズ・ニュース that まさる sent you.

Part A

Complete the following profile of まさる's hero, さいとうたかし, in English.

Profile of _____

Team:

Position:

Date of birth:

Description:

Likes:

Part B

まさる has asked you to meet him at the stadium. Read the directions given on page 63 of the *Textbook* from the station to the stadium. Note them down in English using the note paper below.

Directions from the station to the stadium

-
-
-
-

Imagine that you have returned to your hotel (The Star Hotel, of course!) after the Bay Stars versus Hiroshima Carp baseball game. Making reference to the material on pages 62 and 63 of the *Textbook*, draft a letter in your exercise book（about 200–300 字）to your pen friend みち子.

Details to include:

- your transport to Hiroshima, and from your hotel to the stadium
- your accommodation
- which teams were playing
- date/time
- where it was played
- what you did before the game
- whether or not you saw さいとうたかし
- which team won （かちました）
- the final score （e.g. 5 たい 3 で広島カープがかちました。）

Be sure to use appropriate letter writing style (ref: page 14 of this *Workbook*).

Listen to まさる and たけし chatting about yesterday's baseball game. Indicate whether the statements below are true (**T**) or false (**F**).

> Read the Japanese sentences before listening to the recording. Make notes as you listen.

(a) たけしくんはきのう広島スタジアムでやきゅうのしあいを見ました。　　**T**　**F**

(b) 斉藤せんしゅは横浜ベイ・スターズのピッチャーです。　　**T**　**F**

(c) まさるくんは斉藤せんしゅのサインをもらいました。　　**T**　**F**

(d) まさるくんとたけしくんは、らい週広島スタジアムに行って、つぎのしあいを見ます。　　**T**　**F**

(e) つぎのベイ・スターズのしあいは横浜であります。　　**T**　**F**

第四課　六十四

つかってみよう

22

たけし is taking you on a mystery tour of 広島(しま) centre. While eating a snack at ミスタードーナッツ, he gave you a map with instructions. Read たけし's instructions below and follow the path on the map on page 67 of the *Textbook*. When you find each destination, write the name in Japanese in the space provided below.

ⓐ ミスタードーナッツの前のみちを左に行ってください。一つ目のかどを左にまがってください。まっすぐ行きます。そうすると、二つ目の左がわのかどにあります。

　（　　　　　　　　　）

ⓑ ミスタードーナッツの前のみちを左にまっすぐ行ってください。そうすると、大きいこうさてんがあります。そのこうさてんを左にまがって、大きいみちをまっすぐ行ってください。そして三つ目のこうさてんを右にまがって、まっすぐ行ってください。そうすると、左がわにあります。

　（　　　　　　　　　）

ⓒ ミスタードーナッツの前のみちを右にまっすぐ行ってください。三つ目のみちをわたって、まっすぐ行ってください。二つ目のかどを左にまがります。そうすると、左がわにあります。

　（　　　　　　　　　）

23

Work in pairs to role-play this scenario, referring to the map on page 67 of the *Textbook*.

PERSON A

It is 10 am and you are on your tea break at your part time job at Mr Donuts in downtown Hiroshima. Your shift finishes at 12 pm. Telephone your friend and invite him/her to meet you for lunch at your favourite eating place. (Of course, after working at Mr Donuts all morning, you won't want to meet there.)
Explain how to get to the restaurant.
Make arrangements for the time and place to meet.
End the conversation appropriately.

PERSON B

It is 10 am and you are shopping at one of the department stores in downtown Hiroshima. You receive a call on your mobile phone from your friend who wants to meet you for lunch at a nearby restaurant.
Find out where the restaurant is and the best way to get there.
Make arrangements for the time and place to meet.
End the conversation appropriately.

24

Tom receives a telephone call from ひろ子. She asks him to help her with her English homework and invites him to her house tomorrow. ひろ子 tells Tom how to get to her house from the school. Write notes in English of the directions that she gives him.

> ! Do not worry if you do not understand some of the words in the conversation. Just listen for ひろ子's directions.

25

A Japanese school band will soon visit your school. You are part of the committee which is organising their stay in your town.

Design an A4 page insert to be added to the welcome folder for each member of the band. The insert needs to include:

- a map which identifies your school, their hotel accommodation, the main shops of the area, other important buildings and any interesting local attractions.
- a section with information about your town (eg. it is pretty and quiet/lively etc.)
- possible leisure activities (eg. movies; parks; bicycle rides; beach; sport) and explanations of how to get to these places from their hotel.

You can present the insert either on paper or in electronic form ready for printing (ie using Microsoft Word, Power Point, Publisher or similar software).

おしゃべり TB. P68-69

26

Complete the puzzle by re-writing the given sentences in plain form. When you have finished, the shaded circles will reveal a suggestion for another activity. Write the mystery sentence and its meaning in the space below.

1	やすみましょう
2	きましょう (wear)
3	れんしゅうしましょう
4	うたいましょう
5	えいごをはなしましょう
6	みましょう
7	およぎましょう
8	あるきましょう

Mystery sentence: _____

Meaning: _____

27

Great! A long weekend is coming up and you and your friend are planning to spend time together on Saturday, Sunday and Monday. What will you do? Fill in the following diary with your suggestions. Write complete sentences, using the casual speech style so that you can show your friend.

土曜日	
日曜日	
月曜日	

クイズ!

When you have completed the 「あるこう広島」 unit, try this quiz to see how well you have mastered the key vocabulary, kanji and grammar.

A
Match the Japanese word with its English equivalent. (10 marks)

ゆうびんきょく	road
とおい	traffic light
となり	intersection
しんごう	far
みち	post office
こうさてん	next to
間	bookshop
つぎ	next
パンや	between
本や	bakery

B
Write the reading of the underlined kanji in hiragana. Include any *okurigana*. (5 marks)

1 私のうちはえきに<u>近い</u>です。
   _____

2 <u>一つ目</u>の<u>右</u>がわのみせです。
   _____ _____

3 はなやはぎんこうの<u>後ろ</u>にあります。
   _____

4 この<u>広い</u>みちをまっすぐ行ってください。
   _____

C
Fill in each blank with an appropriate particle. (not は) (5 marks)

1 広島じょうはどこ（　　）ありますか。

2 本どおりモールにみせ（　　）たくさんあります。広島（　　）一番にんきがあります。

3 二つ目のかど（　　）左（　　）まがってください。

D
These sentences make up a conversation between two people. Number the sentences, arranging them in order. (5 marks)

(　) わかりました。ありがとうございました。

(　) ATMはどこですか。

(　) コンビニの前にあります。

(　) ATMですか。ATMは、ええと…

(　) コンビニの前ですね。

E
Write the following sentences in Japanese.

1 Excuse me. Is there a bank around here? (2 marks)
   _____

2 The bank is behind the mall. (2 marks)
   _____

3 Please go straight ahead and cross the bridge. (3 marks)
   _____

4 Turn right at the third corner. (2 marks)
   _____

5 Thank you very much. (1 mark)
   _____

Check your answers against those on page 101. Give yourself a score and read the assessment at the bottom of the page.

第四課　六十八

トラベル

Look at the cover of the fifth 'magazine' on page 71 of the *Textbook*.

- What is the title of this 'magazine'? Do you know another Japanese word which has the same meaning? What do you expect will be included in this 'magazine'?

- What is the とくしゅう of「トラベル」?

- Which island of Japan features in this issue of 「トラベル」?

- Selecting place names from the box below, add labels in hiragana to the map for all the places you know. When you have finished, check your map against the map on page 74 of the *Textbook* and fill in any empty spaces.

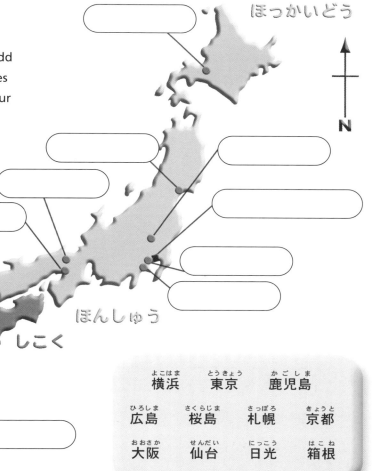

よこはま 横浜	とうきょう 東京	かごしま 鹿児島
ひろしま 広島	さくらじま 桜島	さっぽろ 札幌	きょうと 京都
おおさか 大阪	せんだい 仙台	にっこう 日光	はこね 箱根

69　六十九　第五課

たんご

TB. P72

1 Circle the best alternative. Then check your answers against the vocabulary list on page 72 of the *Textbook*.

a The best time to see cherry blossoms
（はな見）in Japan is:
1. はる
2. なつ
3. あき

b A fun water activity is:
1. スノー・ボード
2. シュノーケリング
3. マウンテン・バイク

c The best place to see こうよう is:
1. ひこうき
2. うみ
3. いなか

d The Japanese word for 'fireworks' is:
1. はなび
2. はな見
3. はな子

2

Complete the following sentences with words from the box below. Each word may be used once only. When you have finished, write out the meaning of each sentence.

a うみに行きました。_____ をしました。
_____

b ふゆにいっしょに山で _____ をしましょう。
_____

c 大阪（おおさか）_____ に行きました。
_____

d 日本人はさくらの木の _____ ではな見をします。
_____

e おんせんに _____ 。気もちがいいです。
_____

スキューバ・ダイビング　　した　　はいります　　スノー・ボード　　じょう

第五課　七十

かんじ TB. P73

3

Practise writing these new kanji in the boxes provided.

千	千						
万	万						
春	春						
夏	夏						
秋	秋						
冬	冬						

4

Try this trick to remember kanji. Design a kanji picture for your favourite season. Working either on a page in your exercise book or in Power Point, write the kanji in the centre and then decorate the kanji using colour and images relating to the season. You could also surround the kanji with Japanese words associated with the season, and even add a sound file that says each word, if you are using Power Point.

71　　　　　　　　　　　　　　　　　　　　　　　　　　七十一　第五課

5

At a かどまつ restaurant the lunchtime menu is written vertically in Japanese. For the benefit of your non-Japanese speaking friends, write the prices in English in the space under each item, eg. ￥450.

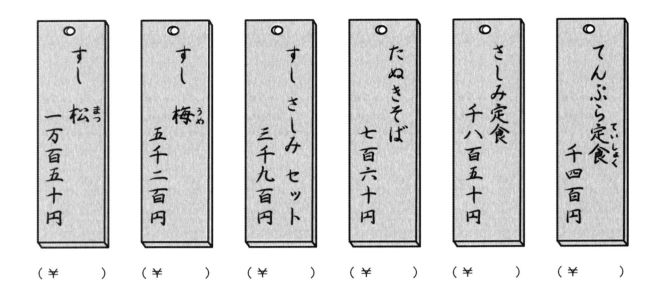

(￥   )   (￥   )   (￥   )   (￥   )   (￥   )   (￥   )

夏休み   TB. P74-75

6

Join each Japanese word to its English equivalent.

二時　　1　　　　a　two hours and fifteen minutes

二時半　2　　　　b　two o'clock

二時間　3　　　　c　twenty minutes

二十分　4　　　　d　two hours

二時間十五分　5　　e　half past two

7

Re-write the following sentences in your exercise book using しか. Then, write the meaning of the new sentences.

a) メルボルンからシドニーまでひこうきで一時間かかります。
b) うちから学校まであるいて五分かかります。
c) まちまでタクシーで十ドルかかりました。
d) きのう四時間ねました。
e) クラスに学生が十五人います。

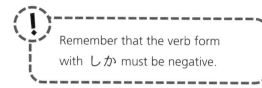

8

Your friend, Sally, is planning to go to Japan during her 夏休み. Because you have spent time in 広島(しま) she has sent you the following email asking for your advice about a trip to 広島. Write a reply in the space below, using information from page 75 of the Textbook.

宛先: southbank@alphalink.com
CC(C):
件名(J): 夏休み

げん気ですか。夏休みに日本に行きたいです。
そして、広島(しま)に行きたいです。東京(とうきょう)からとおいですか。どのぐらいかかりますか。
いくらぐらいですか。eメールをください。サリーより

宛先: sallybrown@hotmail.com
CC(C):
件名(J): 広島

サリーさん、

eメール、ありがとう。

9

You and James are working together to conduct a survey about how your friends will spend their summer holidays. James has already prepared some questions in English.

Part A

Write the survey questions in Japanese in your exercise book.

 Refer to 夏休み on page 74 of the *Textbook* for help forming the questions.

Survey Questions

- Where are you going on your summer holidays?
- Is this place far (or near)?
- How do you get to that place?
- How long does it take you?
- How much does it cost?

Part B

When you have finished, use your questions to interview a student in your Japanese class. Make a note of their answers in Japanese.

Part C

Write a paragraph in your exercise book, including all the information from your interview. Aim to use some linking words like そして and だから, and some adjectives like おもしろい, たのしい or とおい to make your paragraph interesting.

10

Listen to four people talking about their summer holidays. Complete the table below in English.

	names	destination	transportation	time taken	comments
a	Yoshio				
b	Sachiko				
c	Kooji				
d	Keiko				

11

Anne is writing to her Japanese friend about her trip to 大阪 (おおさか) this weekend. The following is her rough draft for the letter. Anne has forgotten some of the facts of the trip and is not sure of some Japanese words, so she has left some gaps. Look at the Travel Schedule on page 75 of the *Textbook* and help Anne to complete her draft in Japanese.

週まつに大阪(おおさか)に行きます。東京(とうきょう)から大阪(おおさか)までしんかんせんで（　　　　　　　　　）ぐらいかかります。でもひこうきで一時間ぐらい（　　　　　　　　　。）しんかんせんよりひこうきの方が（　　　　　　　　　）です。しんかんせんは（　　　　　円）です。エアーチケットは（　　　　　円）かかります。しんかんせんの方がやすくて、おもしろそうです。だからしんかんせんで行きます。

春の東京(とうきょう)　TB. P76-77

12 P.85

Complete the following sentences with an appropriate verb stem. Then, find these verb stems in the following puzzle. When you have finished, a particle will remain. Complete the sentence below in Japanese using that particle.

a) おてらを _____ にいきます。

b) プールに _____ にいきます。

c) おんせんに _____ にいきます。

d) カラオケにうたを _____ にいきます。

e) 買いものを _____ にいきます。

f) さしみを _____ にいきます。

g) おんがくを _____ にいきます。

週まつに友だちと _____。

13 読書 P84-P85

In your exercise book, write mini conversations (minimum ten lines) with appropriate comments, questions and responses based on the photos. An example is given below, based on the photo of おきなわ.

れい　おきなわ

A: おきなわにいつ行きますか。
B: 夏休みに行きます。ひこうきで行きます。
A: いいですね。どのぐらいかかりますか。
B: ええと… 二時間半ぐらいです。
A: だれと行きますか。
B: かぞくと行きます。
A: 何をしにいきますか。
B: ウェイク・ボードをしにいきます。
A: ああ、そうですか。ウェイク・ボードができますか。
B: はい、できます。マリン・スポーツがとくいです。
A: そうですか。私はあまりできません。

一　しんじゅく

二　山

三　友だちのうち

14

PART A

Listen to あつ子 ask her friend, John, about his plans for a trip to Japan next month. On the map below, write down what he is going to do in each place. Write in either English or Japanese.

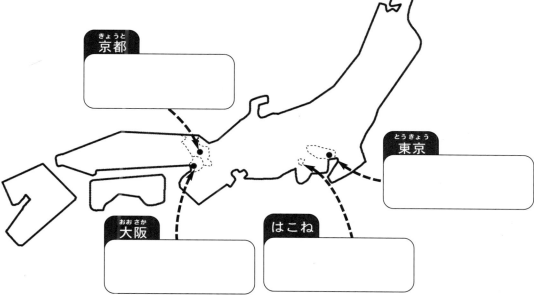

PART B

In your exercise book, write a simple outline of John's trip in Japanese. Summarise where he will go and what he will do in four sentences.

Use the details from the map in **PART A**, above, and the **Verb stem + にいきます** pattern.

15

Listen to a radio advertisement for four top places to visit in Tokyo in spring. Record the details in English in the following table.

Place	Description	Activity
Ginza		
Yoyogi		
Ikebukuro		
Shibuya		

16

Look at the advertisements on page 76 of the *Textbook* for two of the top spots to visit in Tokyo in spring. Complete the activities in your exercise book.

a はらじゅく

1. Write the meaning of the first sentence.
2. Re-write the second sentence to mean 'It's great!' in Japanese.

b しんじゅく

1. Re-write the first sentence to mean 'Let's go to see a new movie' in Japanese.
2. Write the meaning of the second sentence.
3. Write an additional sentence in Japanese – 'There are many big, good cinemas.'

17

「トラベル」magazine plans to have an advertisement for 広島(しま), similar to the Tokyo advertisement on page 76 of the *Textbook*. In your exercise book, write Japanese captions to match the English ones for photo 一 and photo 二. Write both English and Japanese captions for photo 三.

- Let's go to do shopping at the へいわモール
- The shops look interesting
- You can eat at the restaurant
- ひろしまやき is delicious

- Please go to see the Peace Park
- It is very famous
- You can take photographs

第五課 七十八

沖縄でマリン・スポーツ   TB. P78-79

18

Read 沖縄でマリン・スポーツ on page 78 of the *Textbook*. Complete the following activities in your exercise book.

a Find the sentence which means 'I want to try snorkelling'. Then use the pattern to write a new sentence, 'I want to try golf', in Japanese.

b Find the description of the beaches in 沖縄. Use the pattern to write a description in Japanese of a beach you know.

c Look at the cartoon on page 78. Write down three points in English about the boy's summer holiday.

19

Listen to まさき and けんご talking about some activities they would like to try. Circle the activities they talk about.

a para-gliding   mountain-biking   marine sports

b wake-boarding   window shopping   wind-surfing

c flower-viewing   seeing fire-works   seeing autumn colours

d okonomiyaki   hot springs   cheering at baseball

> ⚠ Before you start listening, think about the Japanese for the words you might hear.

20

Your friend, Mary, is writing to her future host family. She has made a note of the following interesting activities, but is unsure of how to say 'I want to try...'. Re-write the sentences for her using 〜てみたいです.

a 書どうをします。
_____

b きものをきます。
_____

c しんかんせんにのります。
_____

d すしを食べます。
_____

21

Congratulations! You have just won the big prize in the lottery! You decide to spend the next two years travelling the world trying lots of new and exciting activities. What will you try to do? Write five sentences in Japanese in your exercise book using the 'try to' pattern.

> ! Can't think beyond the obvious verbs? Check out the verb list in the glossary on pages 106–107 of the *Textbook*.

TB. P 80-81

22

You have a part time job at a travel agency in the city and are required to answer your customers' questions about outdoor tours in Japan. You have just received information about some tours in Japanese. Read アウトドアたいけん on page 80 of the *Textbook* and complete the following tasks.

PART A
Make a note of any words you do not know and look up the meaning either in the vocabulary list at the end of the *Textbook* or *Workbook*, or in your dictionary.

PART B
Consider these scenarios and write your suggestions for each customer in English in your exercise book.

(a) **Customer 1 wants to go to Japan in spring and is interested in some outdoor activities.**

1. Where and what kind of outdoor activities do you suggest?
2. How long does it take to get there from Tokyo?
3. What do you recommend for beginners? What is the cost?

(b) **Customer 2 has travelled to the usual places in Japan several times. This time, he wants to go somewhere different to enjoy his summer holidays.**

1. Where do you suggest, and how long does it take to get there from Tokyo?
2. What is this place like?
3. What kind of outdoor activities do you recommend?
4. What sort of package can you offer? How much does it cost?
5. Explain about renting gear for the activity.

PART C
Design a travel brochure for your English-speaking customers about autumn and/or winter activities in Japan using the information in アウトドアたいけん. The design can be similar to or totally different from that on page 80 in the *Textbook*. You may present your work on paper or in electronic form using Microsoft Word or Publisher or similar software.

第五課 八十

80

23 聞

Listen to some people say what they would like to do in Japan. Decide which season would be most appropriate for each person. Write the number of the conversation next to the most appropriate season.

春（　　　）　　　夏（　　　）　　　秋（　　　）　　　冬（　　　）

> ⚠ Before you listen, read 日本ぶんかたいけん on page 81 of the *Textbook* carefully. Check the words you do not know in the vocabulary list of the *Textbook* or *Workbook*, or in your dictionary.

24 読

Imagine that you have just experienced one of the trips detailed in 日本ぶんかたいけん on page 81 of the *Textbook*. Write a postcard to your family in English describing your trip. Include the following information:

- Where did you go?
- In which season did you go?
- How did you get there and how long did it take?
- What activities did you do?
- How was the trip?

つかってみよう！

25

よしえ, who studied in Australia last year, wrote this letter to her Japanese teacher, Mrs Brown. Read the letter and complete the tasks which follow in your exercise book.

> しっています　from the verb しります (know)
> にぎやか（な）　bustling, lively (as in cities)

ブラウン先生へ、

お元気ですか。ながい間、おてがみを書きませんでした。どうもすみません。日本に帰って、もう一年です。

もうすぐ夏休みです。夏休みにかぞくと一週間沖縄に行きます。沖縄は東京よりあたたかくて、うみがとてもきれいです。スキューバ・ダイビングをしてみたいです。たのしみです。

せん週、こうたさんと浅草に行きました。先生、浅草をしっていますか。ここは私の好きなところです。浅草の浅草寺は東京で一番ふるいおてらです。このおてらの前におもしろいみせがたくさんあります。浅草ではおかしとくつのみせがゆうめいです。週まつにたくさんの人が買いにきます。そして、レストランやえいがかんもたくさんあって、いつもにぎやかです。私たちはたくさんのしゃしんをとりました。このてがみといっしょにおくります。見てください。

では、またてがみを書きます。おからだに気をつけて。

さようなら

6月20日

よしえより

PART A

Answer the following questions in complete Japanese sentences in your exercise book.

a) よしえさんは先生によくてがみを書きますか。
b) 沖縄はどんなところですか。
c) 浅草寺はどんなおてらですか
d) 浅草で何がゆうめいですか。
e) 浅草で、買いもののほかに何ができますか。(other than)

PART B

Using information from よしえ's letter, write a paragraph about 50 字 in length to be included in an advertising brochure about 浅草.

26

Read this postcard and answer the questions below in Japanese.

> きのう、北海道(ほっかいどう)にスキーをしにきました。とてもさむいです。でもゆきはパウダースノーでとても気もちがいいです。今日スノーボードをしてみました。スノーボードのレンタルで四千円かかりました。でも、たのしかったです。
>
> えみより

東京都目黒区
上目黒４－５９
中山時子様

きせつ season

a このはがきはどこからきましたか。
_____

b きせつはいつですか。
_____

c 北海道(ほっかいどう)に何をしに行きましたか。
_____

d スノーボードのレンタルはいくらでしたか。
_____

e だれがこのはがきを書きましたか。
_____

27

Create your own travel brochure in Japanese. Choose a place you would like to visit, or one you have already visited. It may be a city, a town, an island, a theme park or any other place in the world. You may research your chosen place on the internet. Refer to pages 80 and 81 of the *Textbook* for ideas about the type of content to include, and hints for setting out your brochure. Present your brochure either on paper, or in electronic format using software such as Microsoft Word, Power Point or Publisher.

おしゃべり

TB. P86-87

28

See if you can find out why けん's mother is cross. Write the plain form equivalent for each ヒント！ below and a mystery sentence will be revealed in the centre of the puzzle.

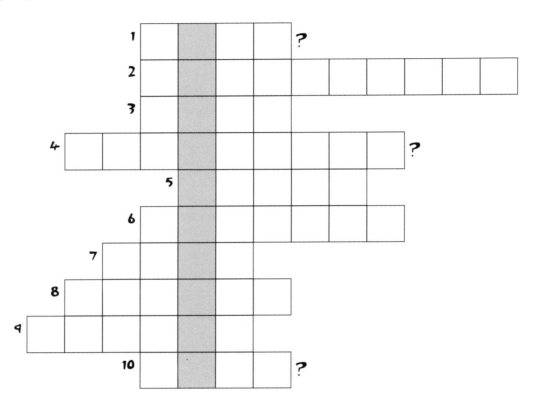

ヒント！

1 食べませんか
2 れんしゅうしませんでした
3 おきません
4 いっしょに行きませんか
5 うたいません
6 はしりませんでした
7 飲みません
8 書きませんでした
9 話しませんでした
10 たちませんか

第五課　八十四

29

a) Refer to けい子's diary on page 87 of the *Textbook* in order to complete this summary of the features of a Japanese diary entry.

- The _____ is written on the top left-hand side of a diary.
- The _____ is written on the top right-hand side of a diary.
- Tick the correct sentence:
  - ☐ In a diary entry, sentence endings are **plain form**.
  - ☐ In a diary entry, sentence endings are です and ます.

b) In the spaces provided, copy how けい子 wrote these sentences in her diary:

1. It was a terrible day.
   _____

2. たけ sang a song.
   _____

3. It was really noisy.
   _____

4. I didn't catch the bus.
   _____

5. I will not walk anymore!
   _____

30

Before going to bed early on the night of her trip to Kyoto, けい子 wrote a quick letter to her grandmother. Complete the gaps in her letter, based on the details she gave in her diary. Notice that she has written her letter in です/ます form.

おばあさんへ、

　今日、京都(きょうと)にえんそくに行きました。東京(とうきょう)から京都(きょうと)まで、しんかんせんで二時間半ぐらい＿＿＿＿＿＿＿＿＿＿＿＿＿。京都(きょうと)のさくらのはなは＿＿＿＿＿＿＿＿＿＿＿＿＿。こうえんでたくさんの人が＿＿＿＿＿＿＿＿＿＿＿＿＿。それから、きれいな清水寺(きよみずでら)を見にいきました。京都(きょうと)はとてもでんとうてきでいい＿＿＿＿＿＿＿＿＿＿＿＿＿。あした、バスで＿＿＿＿＿＿＿＿＿＿＿＿＿＿＿＿＿＿＿。

　　　　　　　　　　　　さようなら

　　４月１日

　　　　　　　　　　　　けい子より

クイズ！ When you have completed the 「トラベル」 unit, try this quiz to see how well you have mastered the key vocabulary, kanji and grammar.

MY SCORE /35 トラベル

A
Write the following English words in Japanese. (5 marks)

1. countryside いなか
2. outdoor アウトドア
3. take time, cost かか
4. snow boarding _____
5. culture _____

B
Write the English equivalent next to the kanji. (5 marks)

1. 三時間 _____
2. 十万五千円 _____
3. 夏休み _____
4. 秋 _____
5. 冬 _____

C

Complete the sentences appropriately using the English hints. (10 marks)

1. うちからまちまでバスで十分しか _____ (take) 。
2. よう子さんのおねえさんに _____ (try to meet) 。
3. 友だちのうちにCDを _____ (went to listen) 。
4. たけくんはアメリカに _____ (study) にきました。
5. わあ、すてきなドレスですね。 _____ (want to try it on) 。

D

Write the following sentences in Japanese.

1. How long does it take from your house to school by car? (4 marks)
   _____

2. It takes only 10 minutes. (2 marks)
   _____

3. I want to try snorkeling in Okinawa. (3 marks)
   _____

4. My friend went to Hokkaido to ski. (3 marks)
   _____

5. Why don't you try okonomiyaki? (3 marks)
   _____

Check your answers against those on Page 101. Give yourself a score and read the assessment at the bottom of the page.

第五課 八十六

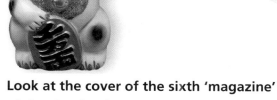

Myしょう来

Look at the cover of the sixth 'magazine' on page 89 of the *Textbook*.

- The focus of this 'magazine' is 「Myしょう来」, meaning 'my future'. What do you want to become in the future? What other plans do you have for the future?

  Make a list in your exercise book of any Japanese words you already know to describe your future plans.

- The Japanese internet uses a lot of modern katakana words, 外来語 (がいらいご), which are often, but not always, based on English words we know. In your exercise book, list all the 外来語 (がいらいご) you can find on page 89 and add the English meanings where you can guess them. Compare your list with a partner.

- まねきねこ, the beckoning cat, is on this cover page. Try to guess its significance to 「Myしょう来」.

たんご　　　　　　　　　　TB. P90

1

Three-hint quiz

Work out the mystery occupations by reading the hints provided. Write your answers in Japanese in the boxes provided. When you have finished, compare your answers with your partner's.

a　人のやくにたつしごとです。
　　びょういんではたらきます。(hospital)
　　いしゃといっしょにはたらきます。

b　人のやくにたつしごとです。
　　子どもが好きです。
　　学校ではたらきます。

c　すうがくやかがくがとくいです。
　　がいこくに行けます。
　　ひこうきが大好きです。

Make up a three-hint quiz for another occupation and challenge your friend.

2
Charades

How about a game of charades? Playing in groups of four or five, take turns to act out different occupations from the list on page 90 of the *Textbook*. See how quickly the other members of your group can say the Japanese word for the occupation which you perform.

かんじ　　TB. P91

3 　書

Practise writing these new kanji in the boxes provided.

上
下
来
先
仕
事

第六課　八十八　88

4 読

クロスワード

Read the kanji in the **よこ** and **たて** hints and complete the crossword in hiragana.

よこ
- 4 近い
- 6 見ます
- 8 千
- 9 来ました
- 11 月曜日
- 14 来月
- 15 新しい
- 17 広い
- 19 仕事
- 20 来る
- 21 読書
- 22 上

たて
- 1 読みます
- 2 私
- 3 万
- 5 火曜日
- 7 好き
- 8 先月
- 10 高い
- 12 後ろ
- 13 下
- 14 来週
- 15 間
- 16 来年
- 17 広島(しま)
- 18 行く

しょう来のゆめ   TB. P92-93

5 聞

Listen to **けん** talk about his family's occupations and complete the table below in English.

	Member of the family	Occupation (current or future)
a		
b		
c		
d		
e		

6

Listen to あきお and よしえ talk about their plans for the future. As you listen fill in the table below in English.

Name	Akio	Yoshie
Age		
Hobby		
Future		

7

Use the information about としえ and けん on page 92 of the *Textbook* to complete the following dialogue.

としえ： けんさんは _____

けん： １６さいです。としえさんは？

としえ： 私は _____

けん： としえさんは _____

としえ： 私はおんがくが大好きです。トロンボーンが _____

> Be a smart learner! Before going to page 92 of the *Textbook* look at the dialogue first, and think about what information you need to complete this dialogue.

けん： そうですか。じゃ、しょう来 _____

としえ： _____ になりたいです。けんさんのしょう来のゆめは何ですか。

けん： ぼくは _____ になりたいです。 _____ プレーしたいです。

8

Read the following passage and circle the correct alternatives.

私はべんきょう（が、を）好きじゃないです。だから大学（に、で）行って、べんきょうしたくないです。私はしょう来（に、の）ゆめ（が、に）あります。ファッション・モデル（を、に）なりたいです。そしてゆうめい（な、で）、お金もち（を、に）なります。おとうとはフランス語（が、を）すこし話せます。しょう来 フランスにフランス語をべんきょうし（を、に）いきます。

You have been asked to write your profile for the しょう来のゆめ page of the school magazine's languages supplement. Use the examples on page 92 of the *Textbook* as a guide and write between 50 and 100 字. You may present your profile either on paper or in electronic format.

チェックリスト: あなたのアルバイトはこれ！ TB. P94-95

Read the three part-time job advertisements on page 95 of the *Textbook* and complete these tasks in your exercise book.

a Answer these questions about 「コーヒーコーナー」 in Japanese sentences.
- どんなアルバイトですか。
- アルバイトは何曜日ですか。
- 時きゅうはいくらですか。
- どんな人がいいですか。

b Answer these questions about 「ベビー・シッター」 in English sentences.
- What sort of person is required for this job?
- When does the family need a baby sitter?
- What are the ages and gender of the children?
- What activities will the baby sitter do?

c Here is けんたろう's profile. Would he be a suitable applicant for the ツアー・ガイド job? Make a list of points for and against in English, and decide whether you would hire him. Be prepared to argue your case.

けんたろう is a university student who has come from Sapporo to study in Tokyo. He is studying English and has been on a working holiday to the United States of America. He likes meeting people and is very outgoing. けんたろう doesn't know Tokyo very well yet. He is looking for a job to help him with his living expenses.

11 読

Complete the check list below, then match your answers against the requirements in each of the advertisements on page 95 of the *Textbook*. Decide which job would suit you most, even if not all requirements are met. Finally, complete the sentence below.

名前 （　　　　　　　　　）（男・女）

① いつ はたらけますか。
- ☐ 週まつ
- ☐ 月曜日～金曜日
- ☐ 金曜日と土曜日

② 何時から、何時まではたらけますか。
- ☐ ごご5時から8時まで
- ☐ ごぜん8時からごご5時まで
- ☐ ごご4時から7時まで

③ あなたはどんな人ですか。
- ☐ あかるくて、クリエイティブ
- ☐ げん気で、会話が上手
- ☐ あかるくて、しゃこうてき

④ フランス語が話せますか。
- ☐ はい
- ☐ いいえ

⑤ 英語がとくいですか。
- ☐ とくい
- ☐ にが手

⑥ とくいなかもくは何ですか。
- ☐ 日本語
- ☐ すう学
- ☐ フランス語

私に一番いいアルバイトは _____ です。

12 聞

You are the assistant to a job recruitment officer who is interviewing candidates for the three part-time jobs advertised on page 95 of the *Textbook*. Your job is to listen to the interviews and make your recommendations about the most suitable job for each candidate. The next candidate is 山田けんじ. In order to help you make the best recommendation, make notes on the form on the right in English or Japanese.

Workネット　アルバイト

____年____月____日

名前	山田けんじ
とくいなかもく	
どんな人	
はたらける時間 (time they can work)	

一番いい仕事：

13

けい子 has submitted the following information about herself. Which of the part-time jobs on page 95 of the *Textbook* do you think she should apply for? Read けい子's information and make your decision. Then record your decision in English in your exercise book, giving five reasons to support it.

私の名前は山下けい子です。十六さいの高校二年生です。しゃこうてきであかるいです。おんがくが大好きです。ひまなとき、ピアノをひいたり、友だちとカラオケをしにいったりします。しゅくだいがたくさんありますが学校が好きです。とくいなかもくはこく語です。英語もフランス語もべんきょうしています。でも、すうがくはにが手です。とてもむずかしくて、つまらないです。
週まつはいつもいそがしいです。ピアノのレッスンが土曜日の八時から十一時まであります。それから、ごご一時から三時までテニスのしあいをします。日曜日はおそくまでねてもいいです。十時からピアノのれんしゅうをします。でも、ごごはひまです。だから、日曜日は休めます。

今月の仕事... ジャーナリスト TB. P 96-97

14

Read the photo stories on page 97 of the *Textbook* and answer the questions in English in the spaces provided.

⊖ ツアー・ガイド
This woman can speak Chinese and German. What are the other two things she likes about being a tour guide?

_____

⊜ たいいくの先生
What other advantage, besides being able to play various sports, does a Physical Education teacher have?

_____

⊜ けいかん
What do you think is the main reason this man became a policeman?

_____

四 コック
According to the caption for photo 四, what are two advantages of being a cook?

_____

15

Join one sentence from the first column with one sentence from the second column to make five logical, complete sentences.

かっこいいくるまが好きですから	a	1	こんばんパーティーに行けません。
新しいじてんしゃが買いたいですが	b	2	書けません。
あしたテストがありますから	c	3	くるまのデザイナーになりたいです。
アイスクリームをたくさん食べましたから	d	4	お金がありません。
日本語が話せますが	e	5	おなかがいたいです。

16

You are gathering information for an article for the 今月の仕事 page of 「Myしょう来」 magazine. A Japanese friend of yours has recorded an interview with three Japanese students. Listen to the interview and complete the table below in English.

Name	Eri	Hiroshi	Yukio
Wants to be…			
Reason			

17

「Myしょう来」 is running a ベストの今月の仕事 competition for its readers. Your challenge is to work in a group, gather relevant information and write it in Japanese. Then design a magazine page, using page 96 of the *Textbook*, 今月の仕事, as a model. Your topic is 先生.

Suggestions for getting information

- Divide the following tasks among members of the group:
  - Interview people who want to be a teacher and ask their reasons.
  - Talk to your Japanese teacher and write her/his profile. This is a good opportunity to speak in Japanese.
  - Ask teachers at your school about the good and bad points of being a teacher.

Hints for the final presentation

- Put the information gathered into Japanese.
- Design the page with photos and pictures, planning where the text will fit in.
- You might like to word-process your entry for the ベストの今月の仕事 competition.

とくしゅう

TB. P98-99

18

Your best friend, さち子, is a huge fan of the Japanese musician, ヨシ. So that you sound knowledgeable next time you see さち子, read the feature article about ヨシ on pages 98 and 99 of the *Textbook* and make some notes in English below.

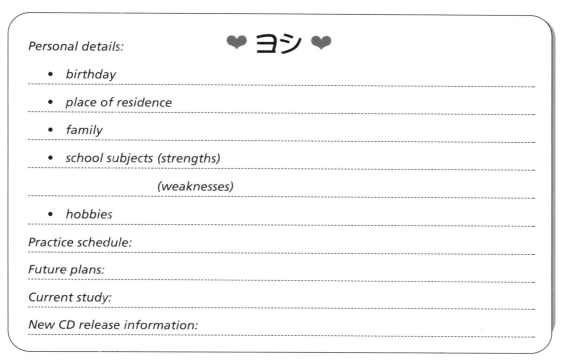

♥ ヨシ ♥

Personal details:
- birthday
- place of residence
- family
- school subjects (strengths)
  (weaknesses)
- hobbies

Practice schedule:

Future plans:

Current study:

New CD release information:

19

Your school's Languages' newsletter is going to run a とくしゅう on world famous musicians. You have been nominated to write an article of 200 – 300 字, about a popular Japanese musician.

PART A
Do some research to find the Japanese musician you want to feature. You could gather this information by talking to Japanese students at your school, looking at magazines, searching the internet.

PART B
Plan your article in English or Japanese. Use the format in question 18 as a guide.

PART C
Write a draft of your article in your exercise book. Refer to page 28 in this *Workbook* for the correct structure of an article. Then ask a friend to check your draft for errors.

PART D
Write your final article of 200 – 300 字 on paper, or present it using Microsoft Word, Power Point or similar software.

つかってみよう！

20

In preparation for a speech about his future plans, けんた has written out what he plans to say.

みなさん、こんばんは。今日、ぼくのしょう来について話します。

ぼくの名前は上田けんたです。今年、高校三年生です。こく語と英語とすうがくとかがくとれきしをべんきょうしています。とくいなかもくはかがくです。そして、すうがくも好きです。でも、エッセーはむずかしいですから、れきしはにが手です。

ぼくはしょう来のゆめが二つあります。どうぶつが大好きですから、じゅういになりたいです。来年、大学にはいって、五年間べんきょうしたいです。

もう一つのゆめはりょこうです。せかいりょこうがしたいです。ヨーロッパやアメリカやオーストラリアに行ってみたいです。きれいなところに行ったり、おいしいものを食べたり、おもしろい人に会ったりしたいです。

ぼくはしょう来がたのしみです。

これでスピーチをおわります。ありがとうございました。

(a) Answer the following questions about けんた's speech in English in your exercise book.

1. What are けんた's subjects this year?
2. What subject is けんた good at?
3. What subject is he not so good at? Why?
4. What career does けんた hope to have in the future?
5. How many years of university study will he have to do?
6. Where does けんた want to travel?
7. What three things does けんた want to do while travelling?

(b) There are several important features of a Japanese speech. The following activities will help you to identify those important features.

1. Underline how けんた starts his speech.
2. Highlight the sentence he uses to introduce the topic of his speech.
3. Circle the sentence which he uses to say his speech is finished.
4. Why does he use ありがとうございました at the end of his speech?

21

Prepare a personal speech about your future plans.

PART A

Make a plan in either English or Japanese (or both) following the structure used by けんた in question 20. Jot down all the things you think you might want to include and sort them into groups which will be your key points. Discuss each key point in a separate paragraph. Use as many separate paragraphs as you need.

PLAN

Speech opening:

Topic:

Paragraph X

Paragraph Y

Paragraph Z

Concluding sentence/s

PART B

When you are ready to write your speech in your exercise book, refer back to question 20 to check the important features to include in a speech. Write a minimum of 200 字, and aim to use a variety of language patterns and known kanji.

PART C

After writing your speech, ask a friend to check it. Then, get together with two or three other students and take turns delivering your speeches.

おしゃべり TB. P 102-103

22

Read the photo story on page 103 of the *Textbook* and complete the following tasks.

a Answer these questions in Japanese. Write complete sentences in your exercise book. You should answer in です／ます form.

1　たけくんはどうしてけいかんになりたいですか。

2　とおるくんはしょう来何をするつもりですか。

3　けんくんは来年何をするつもりですか。

b Using words from the box below, fill in the blanks to complete the following passage.

たけくんはしょう来けいかんに（　　　　　）つもりです。とおるくんは（　　　　　）がとくいです。（　　　　　）でべんきょうするつもりです。けんくんは（　　　　　）ができます。ベトナムを（　　　　　）でりょこう（　　　　　）つもりです。

　　する　　　なる　　　大学　　　コンピューター　　　バック・パック　　　ベトナム語

23

Write three sentences using つもり to explain something you intend to do. Start your sentences with the words given and complete your sentences with です. The first one has been done for you.

a あした、えきの前でたけくんに会うつもりです。

b 来週 _____

c 来年 _____

d しょう来 _____

> ! Refer to pages 108 – 109 of the *Textbook* for a full list of plain form verbs that you could use.

第六課　九十八

クイズ！

You have now completed all six units of this course. Try the final quiz to see how well you have mastered the key vocabulary, kanji and grammar.

A Create a Japanese word by choosing one kanji from the box and writing it in the space provided. Each kanji may be used only once. Then write the meaning of the word in English. (10 marks)

> 読　事　時　来　新　手　語　学　話　生

1　(　　) 校 _____　6　仕 (　　) _____
2　(　　) 書 _____　7　(　　) 聞 _____
3　上 (　　) _____　8　(　　) 年 _____
4　先 (　　) _____　9　電 (　　) _____
5　(　　) 間 _____　10　英 (　　) _____

B Fill in the blanks with an appropriate particle. (5 marks)

1　ぼくは日本語 (　　) とくいです。しょう来、日本の
　会しゃ (　　) はたらきたいです。

2　週まつ、友だちのよしひこくん (　　) 会いました。いっしょに
　まちにえいが (　　) 見 (　　) いきました。

C Join one sentence from the first column with one sentence from the second column, so that they all make sense. (5 marks)

私はテニスが大好きですが　　　　　1　　A　アルバイトをしています。
きみ子さんはあたまがよくてきれいですが　2　　B　あまり上手じゃないです。
あしたすうがくのテストがありますから　3　　C　学校に行きました。
夏休みにりょこうします。お金がいりますから　4　　D　クラスで人気がありません。
今日あたまがいたかったですが、　　　5　　E　テレビを見ません。

99　　　　　　　　　　　　　　　　　　　九十九　第六課

D Complete the following sentences, using the hints given in English. Read the sentences carefully and use the correct form of the verb. (5 marks)

1. おとうとはプロやきゅうのせんしゅに（　　　　　）です。(want to become)
2. よしおくんは来年、カナダに英語を（　　　　　）にいきます。(study)
3. きのうのパーティーで、うたを（　　　　　）たり、ＣＤを（　　　　　）たりしました。(sing, listen)
4. ぼくたちはビールやワインを（　　　　　）はいけませんから、コーラやジュースを飲みました。(drink)
5. すてきなブーツですね。ちょっと（　　　　　）みたいです。(put on)

E Read the following text and answer the questions in English.

> ぼくのあにのケンは大学生です。あたまがいいですが、べんきょうが好きじゃないです。金曜日と土曜日にパンやでアルバイトをしています。時きゅうはいいです。金曜日は９ドルで、土曜日は１２ドルです。ひるごはんが食べられます。いつもおいしいパンが食べられます。でもあさはやくからはたらきますから、たいへんです。アルバイトのお金でかっこいいくるまを買います。

1. Where, and when does he work? (3 marks)

2. How much is he paid hourly? (2 marks)

3. List three good points about the job. (3 marks)

4. What is the disadvantage of this job? (1 mark)

5. What is Ken going to do with the money he has earned? (1 mark)

Check your answers against those on page 101. Give yourself a score and read the assessment at the bottom of the page.

第六課　百

クイズのこたえ

Unit One
a I/me、私、わたし
expensive, tall、高い、たかい
speak、話します、はなします
read、読みます、よみます
write、書きます、かきます
listen、聞きます、ききます
high school student、高校生、こうこうせい
reading、読書、どくしょ
b 1 ひきます 2 読みます 3 つかいます
c 1 めぐみはせが高くてきれいです。 2 たけひとはおしゃれでかみ(or かみのけ)がながいです。 3 ゆうすけはあたまがよくてしゃこうてきです。 4 ゆみはシャイでおとなしいです。
d 1 おはしが (or は) つかえますか。 2 さしみが (or は) 食べられますか。 3 バスのなかでべんきょうができます。 4 十キロはしれます。 5 ドイツ語が話せます。

Unit Two
a もらいます receive、新しい new、おこづかい allowance、ねだん price、べんり convenient
b 1 しんぶん、かいます。 2 おとこのこ、ちゅうがっこう、いって。 3 でんしてちょう、いちばん、あたらしい 4 ともだち、でんわ、はなします
c 1 書きたいです。 2 会いたいです。 3 やさしそう 4 べんりそう
d 1 そのえいがはよさそうです。あした見ましょう。 2 私は土曜日に父とテニスが(or を)したいです。 3 クラシックとロックとどちらの方が好きですか。 4 そのビデオゲームは一番高いです。
e 1 が 2 が 3 に、を 4 に 5 の、が (or を)

Unit Three
a 1 enjoy 2 stay overnight 3 hold 4 rule
b 1 おそく 2 毎日 3 よる 4 せかい
c 1 中、食、飲 2 毎週、帰 3 今年、休
d 1 バスケットボールをしてもいいです。 2 はしってはいけません。 3 （あなたの）コンピューターをつかってもいいですか。 4 せん週まつに、しゅくだいをしませんでした。 5 ふゆ休み（に）、スキーに行ったり、本を読んだりします。
e 1 パーティでうたをうたったり、CDを聞いたりしました。 2 週まつにサイクリングをしたり、えいがを見たりしました。 3 ひる休みにバスケットボールをしたり、友だちと話したりします。 4 日本でしんかんせんにのったり、ペンフレンドに会ったりします。 5 学校にあるいて行ったり、バスで行ったりします。

Unit Four
a ゆうびんきょく post office、とおい far、となり next to、しんごう traffic light、みち road、こうさてん intersection、間 between、つぎ next、パンや bakery、本や bookshop
b 1 ちかい 2 ひとつめ、みぎがわ 3 うしろ 4 ひろい
c 1 に 2 が、で 3 を、に
d 1 ATMはどこですか。 2 ATMですか。ATMは、ええと... 3 コンビニの前にあります。 4 コンビニの前ですね。 5 わかりました。ありがとうございました。
e 1 すみません、このへんにぎんこうは (or が) ありますか。 2 ぎんこうはモールの後ろにあります。(or 後ろです。) 3 まっすぐ行って、はしをわたってください。 4 三つ目のかどを右にまがってください。 5 ありがとうございました。(or どうもありがとう。)

Unit Five
a 1 いなか 2 アウトドア 3 かかります 4 スノーボード 5 ぶんか
b 1 three hours 2 105 000 yen 3 summer holiday 4 autumn 5 winter
c 1 かかりません。 2 会ってみます。 3 聞きにいきました。 4 べんきょうし 5 きてみたいです。
d 1 あなたのうちから学校までくるまでどのぐらいかかりますか。 2 十分しかかかりません。 3 おきなわでシュノーケリングをしてみたいです。 4 私の友だちはほっかいどうにスキーをしにいきました。 5 おこのみやきを食べてみませんか。

Unit 6
a 1 学校 school 2 読書 reading 3 上手 good at 4 先生 teacher 5 時間 time 6 仕事 job 7 新聞 newspaper 8 来年 next year 9 電話 telephone 10 英語 English
b 1 が、で 2 に、を、に
c 1-b 2-d 3-e 4-a 5-c
d 1 なりたい 2 べんきょうし 3 うたっ、聞い 4 飲んで 5 はいて
e 1 at a bakery, on Fridays and Saturdays 2 nine dollars on Friday and twelve dollars on Saturday 3 good pay, free lunch, delicious bread 4 He has to work from early morning. 5 buy a cool car.

Score and Assessment

35–29	おめでとう！You have a great understanding of the new language in this unit. You have developed good learning skills. Keep it up!
28–22	Pretty good, but it is time to brush up on the difficult areas. Check the たんご and かんじ pages of each unit. Then write out the words and かんじ you forgot. For grammar help, refer to the Glossary at the back of the *Textbook* for examples of how to say things in Japanese.
21–0	Time for serious action! Choose one of the hints from pages 2, 3, 18 or 19 to help you learn Japanese words and かんじ. Find the spelling and meaning of words in the vocabulary list at the back of this book. For help in making Japanese sentences, refer to the Glossary at the back of the *Textbook* which gives examples of sentences in English and Japanese.

日本語 – 英語

あ

ATM　ATM
あいだ〔間〕　in between
アイドル　idol
アウトドア　outdoor
あかるい　cheerful, bright
あき〔秋〕　autumn
アジア　Asia
あたたかい　warm
あたまがいい　smart, intelligent
あたらしい〔新しい〕　new
あなた　you
アニメ　animation, cartoon
ある〜　one 〜
あるきます　walk
アルコール　alcohol
アルバイト　part-time job
アルバイトをします　have a part-time job

い

eメール　email
いきたくない〔行きたくない〕　don't want to go
いけません　don't, must not
いしゃ　doctor
いちご　strawberry
いちばん〔一番〕　number 1, best, most, ... est
いつも　always
いなか　countryside
いや（な）　horrible
いります　need
いわぶろ　stone baths
インターネット　internet
インフォメーション　information
インプット　input

う

ウィンド・サーフィン　wind surfing
ウィンドー・ショッピング　window shopping
うえ〔上〕　above
ウェア　wear
ウェイク・ボード　wake boarding
うしろ〔後ろ〕　behind
うみ　beach, sea
うらない　horoscope

え

え　picture, painting
エアーチケット　air ticket
エレベーター　elevator
エンジニア　engineer
えんそうします　perform (musically)

お

おうえんしてください　please support
おおかみ　wolf
おかねもち〔お金もち〕　rich person
おくります　send
おこづかい　allowance, pocket money
おこのみやき　Japanese-style pancake
おしゃれ（な）　trendy, fashionable
おそく　late
おとな〔大人〕　adult
おとなしい　quiet, reserved
おめでとう　congratulations
オリンピック　Olympic Games
おんせん　hot springs

か／が

か　or
が　but
カーナビ　car navigation system
ガールフレンド　girlfriend
がいこく　foreign countries
かいしゃいん〔会しゃいん〕　company employee
かいます〔買います〕　buy
かえります〔帰ります〕　go home
かかります　take time, cost
かきます〔書きます〕　write
かきます　draw, paint
かしゅ　singer
かど　corner
カフェ　cafe
カメラマン　cameraman
かります　borrow
カルビまん　Karubiman; brand of steamed bun filled with spicy beef
〜がわ　〜side
〜かん〔間〕　period of time
がーん　Oh! What a shock!
かんごふ　nurse

き／ぎ

ききます〔聞きます〕　ask, listen, hear
きそく　rule
きびしい　strict, harsh
きます〔来ます〕　come
きもちがいい〔気もちがいい〕　feel good
キャラクター　character
きょうしつのそと　outside the classroom
キロ　kilometre
ぎんこう　bank
ぎんこういん　banker

く／ぐ

グッズ　goods
〜ぐらい　about, approximately
グラフィック・デザイナー　graphic designer
クリエイティブ（な）　creative
クレープ　crepe
クレジットカード　credit card
くろひょう　black leopard

け／げ

けいかん　police officer
けいたいでんわ〔けいたい電話〕　mobile phone
ゲームセンター　game centre
けしょうひん　cosmetics
げんき（な）〔げん気（な）〕　healthy, lively

こ／ご

コアラ　koala
コーチ　coach
こうこう〔高校〕　senior high school
こうこうせい〔高校生〕　senior high school student
こうさてん　intersection
こうむいん　public servant
こうよう　autumn colours
こじか　young deer
こたえてください　please answer
コック　chef, cook
こと　thing (abstract)
ことし〔今年〕　this year
このへん　around here
こみ　included
これでおわります　I'll finish here, this is the end
こんげつ〔今月〕　this month
コンビニ　convenience store
コンピューター・プログラマー　computer programmer

日本語 – 英語

さ／ざ
サイン autograph, signature
さがします look for, search
さくら cherry blossom
さる monkey

し／じ
しか（～ません） only (with negative verb)
しかく qualifications, requirements
じかん〔時間〕 hour, time
じきゅう〔時きゅう〕 hourly rate of pay
しごと〔仕事〕 work, employment
じしょ〔じ書〕 dictionary
した〔下〕 under
しでん〔市電〕 tram
ジャーナリスト journalist
ジャーナリズム journalism
シャイ（な） shy
しゃこうてき（な） sociable
じゅうい veterinarian
しゅうまつ〔週まつ〕 weekend
じゅぎょう class
シュノーケリング snorkelling
しゅふ housewife
～じょう ～ castle
じょうず（な）〔上手（な）〕 good at
じょうだん joke
じょうば horse riding
しょうらい〔しょう来〕 future
しょどう〔書どう〕 calligraphy
しりたい want to know
シルバー（の） silver
しんごう traffic lights
しんせつ（な） kind

す／ず
すいか watermelon
すいじょうスキー〔水上スキー〕 water skiing
すいます（たばこを） smoke
スキージャンプ ski jump
スキューバ・ダイビング scuba diving
スクーター scooter
スケジュール schedule
スタジアム stadium
ストレッチ stretch
スノー・ボード snow boarding
スピーチ speech
スリル thrill

せ／ぜ
せかい world
せん〔千〕 thousand
せんしゅうまつ〔先週まつ〕 last weekend
せんせい〔先生〕 teacher

そ／ぞ
ぞう elephant
そうじ cleaning
そうすると then (after doing that)
そして and then
そと outside
そんなとき〔そんな時〕 in that case

た／だ
たい versus
だいがく〔大学〕 university
だいく builder, carpenter
たいけん personal experience
だいじょうぶ OK
たいへん（な） terrible, very difficult
たかい〔高い〕 expensive, high, tall
だから therefore
ただ free of charge
たとえば for example
たなばたまつり Star Festival celebrated on the 7th of July
たぬき raccoon dog
たのしみです I'm looking forward to it
たのしみます enjoy
たばこ cigarette
だめ don't, must not

ち
チータ cheetah
ちかい〔近い〕 near, close
ちかく〔近く〕 nearby
チャンピオン champion
～ちゅうに〔～中に〕 during

つ／づ
ツアー・ガイド tour guide
つかいます use
つき〔月〕 a month
つぎ next
つきます arrive
つもり intend

て／で
デート date
でかけます go out, leave
できます can do, can play
てちょう〔手ちょう〕 organiser
てん point
てんいん (shop) assistant
でんし〔電子〕 electronic
でんとうてき（な） traditional

と／ど
トイレ toilet, lavatory
どうぶつ animal
とおい far
とくい（な） good at, skillful (one's strong point, special skill)
とくしゅう feature
どくしょ〔読書〕 reading
とくに especially
どこでも everywhere
ところ place
ところで by the way
どちら which (of 2 things)
となり next to, neighbouring
どのぐらい how long, how much
とまります stay (overnight)
ともだちができます〔友だちができます〕 make friends
とら tiger
どれ which (for more than 2 things)
トロンボーン trombone
どんなこと what kind of things

な
ナイタースキー night skiing
なか〔中〕 middle, in, inside, among
なつ〔夏〕 summer
など etc.
なまちゃ brand of chilled green tea
なります become

に
にがて(な)〔にが手(な)〕 not so good at (and don't like much), a weak point
にく meat
～について about
にわし gardener

日本語 – 英語

ね
ねだん price

の
のうふ farmer
のみます〔飲みます〕 drink

は
パーソナル personal
ハードロック hard rock
パープル（の） purple
バイキング buffet
ハイテク（な） hi-tech
はいっています contains
はいります enter, get in, join
パイロット pilot
パウダー・スノー powder snow
ばか（な） stupid
はし bridge
はし chopsticks
はじまります begin, start
はしります run
はたち 20 years old
はたらきます work
バックパック backpack
はなします〔話します〕 speak
はなび fireworks
はなみ〔はな見〕 flower viewing
はなや florist
はやい fast, quick, early
はやく quickly, early
パラ・グライダー paragliding
はる〔春〕 spring
バレエ ballet
ばんごう〔番ごう〕 number
パンや bakery

ひ
ピアス(をします) pierce (e.g., ears)
ビギナー beginner
ひきます play (a stringed instrument)
ひこうき aeroplane
ひさしぶり it's been a while
ひだり〔左〕 left
ひだりがわ〔左がわ〕 left side
ひつじ sheep
ビデオゲーム video game
ひとつめ〔一つ目〕 first
人のやくにたつ仕事 job which helps people
ひろい〔広い〕 wide, spacious

ひろしまやき〔広島やき〕 Hiroshima-style おこのみやき

ふ
フィジオセラピスト physiotherapist
ふたつめ〔二つ目〕 second
ふゆ〔冬〕 winter
プラス plus, add
ぶらぶらします hang out
プラモデル plastic model
フリースタイル freestyle, crawl (swimming stroke)
ブルー（の） blue
プレーしたい want to play
プロのインストラクター professional instructor
プロのスポーツせんしゅ professional athlete
ぶんか culture

へ
ヘアースタイリスト hairstylist
ペガサス Pegasus
ベスト・スポット best spot
へた（な）〔下手（な）〕 not very good at
べんごし lawyer
べんり（な） convenient, useful

ほ
ほう〔方〕 side
ボーイフレンド boyfriend
ボーカル vocals
ホール hall
ほしい want
ほしいもの things you want
ポップス pop music
ほんや〔本や〕 bookshop

ま
まいしゅうまつ〔毎週まつ〕 every weekend
まいにち〔毎日〕 everyday
マウンテン・バイク mountain biking
まがります turn
まじめ（な） serious
まっすぐ straight
までに by, no later than
マリン・スポーツ marine sports
まん〔万〕 ten thousand
まんがきっさ coffee shop with a comic book library

み
みぎ〔右〕 right
みぎがわ〔右がわ〕 right side
みずうみ lake
みたくない〔見たくない〕 don't want to see
みち street, road
みつけた〔見つけた〕 found
みっつめ〔三つ目〕 third

め
メール mail, email
メッセージ message
メルとも〔メル友〕 keypal, e-pal

も
もう already, more
モール mall
モダンなおふろ modern baths
もちます hold
もの thing
もらいます receive

や
や and (others)
やすみ〔休み〕 holiday, break
やすみます〔休みます〕 rest

ゆ
ゆうびんきょく post office
ゆうめいになりたいです want to be famous
ゆめ dream

よ
ようふく clothes
よっかかん〔四日間〕 a four-day period
よみます〔読みます〕 read
より than
よる night

ら
ライオン lion
ライセンス licence

日本語 – 英語／英語 – 日本語

り
リアル（な）　real
リレー　relay
りんご　apple

れ
レギュレーター　regulator
レッスン　lesson

わ
わすれた　forgot
わたし〔私〕　I, me, myself
わたしたち〔私たち〕　we, us
わたります　cross over

A
about　〜について
above　うえ〔上〕
add, plus　プラス
adult　おとな〔大人〕
aeroplane　ひこうき
air ticket　エアーチケット
alcohol　アルコール
allowance, pocket money　おこづかい
already, more　もう
always　いつも
among, in, inside, middle　なか〔中〕
and (others)　や
and then　そして
animal　どうぶつ
animation, cartoons　アニメ
(please) answer　こたえてください
apple　りんご
approximately, about　〜ぐらい
around here　このへん
arrive　つきます
Asia　アジア
ask, listen, hear　ききます〔聞きます〕
assistant (shop)　てんいん
ATM　ＡＴＭ (エイティエム)
autograph, signature　サイン
autumn　あき〔秋〕
autumn colours　こうよう

B
backpack　バックパック
bakery　パンや
ballet　バレエ
bank　ぎんこう
banker　ぎんこういん
beach, sea　うみ
become　なります

begin, start　はじまります
beginner　ビギナー
behind　うしろ〔後ろ〕
best, most, ...est, number 1　いちばん〔一番〕
best spot　ベスト・スポット
black leopard　くろひょう
blue　ブルー(の)
bookshop　ほんや〔本や〕
borrow　かります
boyfriend　ボーイフレンド
break, holiday　やすみ〔休み〕
bridge　はし
bright, cheerful　あかるい
buffet　バイキング
builder, carpenter　だいく
but　でも、が
buy　かいます〔買います〕
by, no later than　までに
by the way　ところで

C
cafe　カフェ
calligraphy　しょどう〔書どう〕
can do　できます
can play　できます
car navigation system　カーナビ
carpenter, builder　だいく
cartoon, animation　アニメ
~ castle　〜じょう
champion　チャンピオン
character　キャラクター
cheerful, bright　あかるい
cheetah　チータ
chef, cook　コック
cherry blossom　さくら
chilled green tea (brand name)　なまちゃ

chopsticks　はし
cigarette　たばこ
class　じゅぎょう
cleaning　そうじ
close, near　ちかい〔近い〕
clothes　ようふく
coach　コーチ
coffee shop with a comic book library　まんがきっさ
come　きます〔来ます〕
company employee　かいしゃいん〔会しゃいん〕
computer programmer　コンピューター・プログラマー
congratulations　おめでとう
contains　はいっています
convenience store　コンビニ
convenient, useful　べんり(な)
corner　かど
cosmetics　けしょうひん
cost, take time　かかります
countryside　いなか
crawl, freestyle (swimming stroke)　フリースタイル
creative　クリエイティブ(な)
credit card　クレジットカード
crepe　クレープ
cross over　わたります
culture　ぶんか

D
date　デート
dictionary　じしょ〔じ書〕
doctor　いしゃ
don't, must not　だめ
don't, must not　いけません
don't want to go　いきたくない〔行きたくない〕

105　　百五

英語 – 日本語

don't want to see みたくない〔見たくない〕
draw, paint かきます
dream ゆめ
drink のみます〔飲みます〕
during、〜ちゅうに〔〜中に〕

E

early, fast, quick はやい
early, quickly はやく
electronic でんし〔電子〕
elephant ぞう
elevator エレベーター
email eメール
email, mail メール
employment, work しごと〔仕事〕
engineer エンジニア
enjoy たのしみます
enter, get in, join はいります
especially とくに
etc. など
everyday まいにち〔毎日〕
every weekend まいしゅうまつ〔毎週まつ〕
everywhere どこでも
expensive, high, tall たかい〔高い〕
experience (personal) たいけん

F

far とおい
farmer のうふ
fashionable, trendy おしゃれ(な)
fast, quick, early はやい
feature とくしゅう
feel good きもちがいい〔気もちがいい〕
finish おわります
fireworks はなび
first ひとつめ〔一つ目〕
florist はなや
flower viewing はなみ〔はな見〕
for example たとえば
foreign countries がいこく
forgot わすれた
found みつけた〔見つけた〕
free of charge ただ

freestyle, crawl (swimming stroke) フリースタイル
function きのう
future しょうらい〔しょう来〕

G

game centre ゲームセンター
gardener にわし
get in, enter, join はいります
girlfriend ガールフレンド
go home かえります〔帰ります〕
go out, leave でかけます
good at じょうず(な)〔上手(な)〕
good at, skillful (one's strong point, special skill) とくい(な)
goods グッズ
graphic designer グラフィック・デザイナー

H

hairstylist ヘアースタイリスト
hall ホール
hang out ぶらぶらします
hard rock (music) ハードロック
harsh, strict きびしい
have a part-time job アルバイトします
healthy, lively げんき(な)〔げん気(な)〕
hear, ask, listen ききます〔聞きます〕
hi-tech ハイテク(な)
high, expensive, tall たかい〔高い〕
hold もちます
holiday, break やすみ〔休み〕
horoscope うらない
horrible いや(な)
horse riding じょうば
hot springs おんせん
hour, time じかん〔時間〕
hourly rate of pay じきゅう〔時きゅう〕
housewife しゅふ
how long, how much どのぐらい

I

I, me, myself わたし〔私〕
idol アイドル
in, inside, among, middle なか〔中〕

in between あいだ〔間〕
in that case そんなとき〔そんな時〕
included こみ
information インフォメーション
input インプット
intelligent, smart あたまがいい
intend つもり
internet インターネット
intersection こうさてん

J

job which helps people 人のやくにたつ仕事
join, enter, get in はいります
joke じょうだん
journalism ジャーナリズム
journalist ジャーナリスト

K

Karubiman; brand of steamed bun filled with spicy beef カルビまん
keypal, e-pal メルとも〔メル友〕
kilometre キロ
kind しんせつ(な)
know しります、しっています
koala コアラ

L

lake みずうみ
last weekend せんしゅうまつ〔先週まつ〕
late おそく
lavatory, toilet トイレ
lawyer べんごし
leave, go out でかけます
left ひだり〔左〕
left side ひだりがわ〔左がわ〕
lesson レッスン
licence ライセンス
lion ライオン
listen, hear, ask ききます〔聞きます〕
lively, healthy げんき(な)〔元気(な)〕
look for, search さがします

英語 - 日本語

M
- mail, email　メール
- make friends　ともだちができます〔友だちができます〕
- mall　モール
- marine sports　マリン・スポーツ
- me, myself, I　わたし〔私〕
- meat　にく
- message　メッセージ
- middle, in, inside, among　なか〔中〕
- mobile phone　けいたいでんわ〔けいたい電話〕
- modern baths　モダンなおふろ
- monkey　さる
- month, a month　つき〔月〕
- more, already　もう
- most, best, ...est, number 1　いちばん〔一番〕
- mountain biking　マウンテン・バイク
- must not, don't　いけません

N
- near, close　ちかい〔近い〕
- nearby　ちかく〔近く〕
- need　いります
- new　あたらしい〔新しい〕
- next　つぎ
- next to, neighbouring　となり
- night　よる
- night skiing　ナイタースキー
- no later than, by　までに
- not so good at (and don't like much), a weak point　にがて(な)〔にが手(な)〕
- not very good at　へた(な)〔下手(な)〕
- number　ばんごう〔番ごう〕
- number 1, best, most, ...est　いちばん〔一番〕
- nurse　かんごふ

O
- Oh! What a shock!　がーん
- Olympic Games　オリンピック
- OK　だいじょうぶ
- okonomiyaki (Hiroshima-style)　広島やき
- one　～ある～
- one month　いっかげつ〔一ヵ月〕
- only (with negative verb)　しか(～ません)
- or　か
- organiser　てちょう〔手ちょう〕
- outdoor　アウトドア
- outside　そと
- outside the classroom　きょうしつのそと

P
- pancake (Japanese-style)　おこのみやき
- paragliding　パラ・グライダー
- part-time job　アルバイト
- Pegasus　ペガサス
- perform (musically)　えんそうします
- period of time　～かん〔間〕
- personal　パーソナル
- physiotherapist　フィジオセラピスト
- picture, painting　え
- pierce (e.g., pierce ears)　ピアス(をします)
- pilot　パイロット
- place　ところ
- plane　ひこうき
- plastic model　プラモデル
- play (a stringed instrument)　ひきます
- please answer　こたえてください
- please support　おうえんしてください
- plus, add　プラス
- pocket money, allowance　おこづかい
- point　てん
- police officer　けいかん
- pop music　ポップス
- post office　ゆうびんきょく
- powder snow　パウダー・スノー
- price　ねだん
- professional athlete　プロのスポーツせんしゅ
- professional instructor　プロのインストラクター
- public servant　こうむいん
- purple　パープル(の)

Q
- qualifications, requirements　しかく
- quick, early, fast　はやい
- quiet, reserved　おとなしい

R
- raccoon dog　たぬき
- read　よみます〔読みます〕
- reading　どくしょ〔読書〕
- real　リアル
- receive　もらいます
- regulator　レギュレーター
- relay　リレー
- requirements, qualifications　しかく
- reserved, quiet　おとなしい
- rest　やすみます〔休みます〕
- rich person　おかねもち〔お金もち〕
- right　みぎ〔右〕
- right side　みぎがわ〔右がわ〕
- road, street　みち
- rule　きそく
- run　はしります

S
- schedule　スケジュール
- scooter　スクーター
- scuba diving　スキューバ・ダイビング
- sea, beach　うみ
- search, look for　さがします
- second　ふたつめ〔二つ目〕
- send　おくります
- senior high school　こうこう〔高校〕
- senior high school student　こうこうせい〔高校生〕
- serious　まじめ(な)
- sheep　ひつじ
- shop assistant　てんいん
- shy　シャイ(な)
- side　ほう〔方〕
- ~side　～がわ
- signature, autograph　サイン
- silver　シルバー(の)
- singer　かしゅ
- ski jump　スキージャンプ

英語 – 日本語

skillful, good at (one's strong point, special skill) とくい(な)
smart, intelligent あたまがいい
smoke （たばこを）すいます
snorkelling シュノーケリング
snow boarding スノー・ボード
sociable しゃこうてき(な)
some ~, one ~ ある～
spacious, wide ひろい〔広い〕
speak はなします〔話します〕
speech スピーチ
spring はる〔春〕
stadium スタジアム
Star Festival celebrated on the 7th of July たなばたまつり
start, begin はじまります
stay (overnight) とまります
stone baths いわぶろ
straight まっすぐ
strawberry いちご
street, road みち
stretch ストレッチ
strict, harsh きびしい
stupid ばか(な)
summer なつ〔夏〕
support おうえんします

T

take time, cost かかります
tall, expensive, high たかい〔高い〕
teacher せんせい〔先生〕
ten thousand まん〔万〕
terrible, very difficult たいへん(な)
than より
then (after doing that) そうすると
therefore だから
thing (abstract) こと
thing もの
things you want ほしいもの
third みっつめ〔三つ目〕
this month こんげつ〔今月〕
this year ことし〔今年〕
thousand せん〔千〕
thrill スリル
tiger とら
time, hour じかん〔時間〕
toilet, lavatory トイレ
tour guide ツアー・ガイド
traditional でんとうてき(な)
traffic lights しんごう
tram しでん〔市電〕
trendy, fashionable おしゃれ(な)
trombone トロンボーン
turn まがります
twenty years old はたち

U

under した〔下〕
us, we わたしたち〔私たち〕
use つかいます
useful, convenient べんり(な)

V

versus たい
very difficult, terrible たいへん(な)
veterinarian じゅうい
video game ビデオゲーム
vocals ボーカル

W

wake boarding ウェイク・ボード
walk あるきます
want ほしい
want to be famous ゆうめいになりたいです
want to know しりたい
want to play プレーしたい
warm あたたかい
water skiing すいじょうスキー〔水上スキー〕
watermelon すいか
we, us わたしたち〔私たち〕
wear ウェア
weekend しゅうまつ〔週まつ〕
what kind of things どんなこと
which (for more than 2 things) どれ
which (of 2 things) どちら
wide, spacious ひろい〔広い〕
wind surfing ウィンド・サーフィン
window shopping ウィンドー・ショッピング
winter ふゆ〔冬〕
wolf おおかみ
work はたらきます
work, employment しごと〔仕事〕
world せかい
write かきます〔書きます〕

Y

you あなた
young deer こじか